2012
A Clarion Call

Your Soul's Purpose
in Conscious Evolution

NICOLYA CHRISTI

Bear & Company
Rochester, Vermont • Toronto, Canada

Bear & Company
One Park Street
Rochester, Vermont 05767
www.BearandCompanyBooks.com

Text paper is SFI certified

Bear & Company is a division of Inner Traditions International

Library of Congress Cataloging-in-Publication Data

Christi, Nicolya.
  2012 : a clarion call : your soul's purpose in conscious evolution / Nicolya Christi.
    p. cm.
  Includes index.
  Summary: "A step-by-step guide to creating a sustainable global shift in consciousness starting with an inner-world shift at the personal level"—Provided by publisher.
  ISBN 978-1-59143-129-9 (pbk.)
  1. Spiritual life—Miscellanea. 2. Two thousand twelve, A.D. I. Title. II. Title: Twenty twelve. III. Title: Two thousand twelve.
  BF1999.C555 2011
  202'.3—dc22

                           2010052397

Printed and bound in the United States by Lake Book Manufacturing
The text paper is SFI certified. The Sustainable Forestry Initiative® program promotes sustainable forest management.

10 9 8 7 6 5 4 3 2 1

Text design and layout by Virginia Scott Bowman
This book was typeset in Garamond Premier Pro with Torino and Gill Sans as display typefaces

To send correspondence to the author of this book, mail a first-class letter to the author c/o Inner Traditions • Bear & Company, One Park Street, Rochester, VT 05767, and we will forward the communication; or visit the author's website at **www.nicolyachristi.com** or **www.worldshiftmovement.org**.

Sometimes our light goes out but is blown again into a flame by an encounter with another human being.

ALBERT SCHWEITZER

This book is dedicated to my beloved friend, mentor, and inspiration, Wendy Webber, the wind beneath my wings. With my deepest love and gratitude for being instrumental in rekindling the inner light within me.

For all, I wish an inspired and transformational journey as we head ever closer to the great Shift of Ages. May all humanity, all sentient beings, and all life on Earth come to live in unconditional love, joy, peace, and harmony.

May we stand together in unity and manifest the Golden Age that ancient elders have prophesied to unfold from the winter solstice of 2012.

May we co-create a new world built upon love, peace, and wisdom as we cross the December 21, 2012, threshold, fulfilling the Mayan prophecy that at this time humanity will enter into a "thousand years of peace."

DIVINE DISPENSATION

Channeled through Nicolya Christi during the writing of
2012: A Clarion Call

Whatever is stopping you, whatever resistances rise to the surface when your true Self tries to emerge, whatever it is that stands between you and your soul's higher purpose, know this: a Divine Dispensation will be awarded to all who respond to this urgent Call from the higher dimensions. Until now, to move through your human personality disorders, dysfunctions, wounding, and karma would have required several years of deep introspection, self-reflection, and contemplation.

We say unto you, dearly beloved seekers of light, love, peace, and truth—

For every soul who is willing to put aside their personal issues to serve the Earth and all life forms, for those who are willing to dedicate themselves to the great cause in the coming years with unwavering commitment, know this: through your dedicated service for the higher good and for your devotion to Spirit in the specific time span between the year 2009 to the close of the year 2012, the burdensome weight of your karma will be lifted from your soul as you cross the threshold of 21 December 2012.

And so it is . . .

Contents

The WorldShift 2012 Declaration

A Declaration of Global Emergency and Emergence

By Ervin Laszlo and David Woolfson

THE CRISIS AND THE OPPORTUNITY

There is no doubt that we are now in a state of global emergency. This unprecedented worldwide crisis is a symptom of a much deeper problem: the current state of our consciousness; how we think about ourselves and our world. We have the urgent need, and now the opportunity, for a complete rethink: to reconsider our values and priorities, to understand our interconnectedness, and to shift to a new direction, living in harmony with nature and each other.

Every person, community, and society in the world is already, or will soon be, affected by the global crisis, through climate change, economic breakdown, ecosystem breakdown, population pressure, food and water shortages, resource depletion, and nuclear and other threats. If we continue on our present unsustainable path, by midcentury the Earth could become largely uninhabitable for human and countless other forms of life. However, total-system collapse could occur much sooner, caused by ecocatastrophes or escalating wars triggered by religious, geopolitical, or resource conflicts.

These threats are real. The underlying causes of the present worldwide crisis have been building momentum for decades and could soon become irreversible. Estimates of when the point of no return will be reached have been reduced from the end of the century, to midcentury, to the next twenty years, and recently to the next five to ten years.

The window of opportunity for shifting our current path and breaking through to a peaceful and sustainable world may be no more than a few years from now. This timeline coincides with the many forecasts and prophecies that speak of the ending of the current cycle of human life on this planet, and the possible dawning of a new consciousness, by the end of the year 2012.

Today, forward-thinking groups and individuals all over the world are addressing the many opportunities presented at this critical time. Designs for sustainable systems, structures, and technologies are being developed and implemented in all sectors, at all levels, and in every society. This global awakening is a hopeful sign of the vitality of the human spirit and our ability to respond to the dangers we now face with insight and creativity.

The totality of our current efforts does not yet match the scope, scale, and urgency of the necessary transformation. But if we collaborate and act with vision, foresight, and commitment we can lay the foundations of a global community that is peaceful, just, and sustainable. We may then ensure our survival and well-being, as well as that of future generations. While the window of time is still open, our top priority as global citizens is to accelerate our evolutionary shift to a planetary consciousness and, together, co-create this new world and a positive future for humanity.

AN URGENT CALL

We accordingly issue this urgent call to all the peoples of the world to deepen our awareness of both the dangers and the opportunities of the present global crisis. We declare our firm commitment to work together to bring about a timely and positive WorldShift for the survival and well-being of the entire human community and the flourishing of all life on Earth.

To join us or sign the WorldShift Declaration, please visit

www.worldshiftmovement.org

Foreword

Affirming and Inviting All of Us to Join Nicolya Christi's Clarion Call

2012: A Clarion Call is a guide to the evolution of the new human. It places us in the precise moment of our "metamorphosis."

As "imaginal cells" we are no longer networking and resonating in the body of the dying societal caterpillar.* We are propelled by the deeper design of creation to the period of metamorphosis, of radical change, when we reassemble and recreate ourselves anew in the form of the yet unseen body of the societal butterfly. Nicolya singles out December 21, 2012, as the due date for this appearance of the new.

What happens in this period of metamorphosis? What are we going through right NOW? This is Real Time Evolution. The great mystics

---

*In an interview with journalist Scott London, innovative geobiologist Elisabet Sahtouris offers "imaginal cells" as a beautiful metaphor for what is happening now: "In metamorphosis, within the body of the caterpillar little things that biologists call imaginal discs or imaginal cells begin to crop up in the body of the caterpillar. They aren't recognized by the immune system so the caterpillar's immune system wipes them out as they pop up. It isn't until they begin to link forces and join up with each other that they get stronger and are able to resist the onslaught of the immune system, until the immune system itself breaks down and the imaginal cells form the body of the butterfly." (www .scottlondon.com/interviews/sahtouris.html)

and seers of humanity have heralded and prefigured this metamorphosis, telling us that it is coming. But none of us on this Earth have been through this exact phase change before, when the old is dying and the new is not quite born. It is our most dangerous period.

Nicolya Christi is our guide through this evolutionary world shift, one of the best I have ever encountered. She lovingly and clearly outlines phases of ascension and transmutation based on her own experience, informed by wide knowledge of the mystic traditions of all cultures. She takes us by the hand and draws us into the unknown field of our own transformation, paving the way for us like a human angel guiding, supporting, and attracting us forward.

As one who has experienced some of these evolutionary signals of species-wide evolution myself, I am grateful to Nicolya for her wisdom and love. She helps us realize we are not alone, no matter how new we may be.

BARBARA MARX HUBBARD,
PRESIDENT OF THE FOUNDATION FOR CONSCIOUS EVOLUTION

Acknowledgments

I offer my love and gratitude to:

"The Luminous Ones," those divine Beings who dwell in the higher dimensions. You are my constant beloved companions, teachers, and dearest friends. It is you who have brought this book to the world. I have merely been your humble channel. You have my deepest love, devotion, and gratitude.

Mahatma Gandhi. Thank you for teaching me about love, nonviolent communication, peace, humility, passive resistance, and truth.

The Master Omraam Mikhael Aivanhov. Thank you for reminding me of the importance of always cultivating purity, love, wisdom, and beauty.

Miracle, the Sacred White Buffalo. My deepest love and gratitude for the blessing and miracle of your having graced my life with your presence. Thank you for your presence and guidance in the conception, labor, and birthing of *2012: A Clarion Call*. Your spirit is held deep in my heart and I give thanks for you every day. This book has come into manifestation only because of you.

Wendy Webber. Thank you for loving me unconditionally and imprinting that as a felt experience within my whole being. This has made it possible for me to offer that toward myself and to others. Your infinite capacity for *being* unconditional love, peace, wisdom, and humility continues to exert the most profound influence on my thoughts, words, actions, and deeds. You are my greatest living inspiration; without knowing you it would not have been possible for this book to have been channeled through my heart. Every step I take in my personal and vocational life has your own footprint just ahead of it.

Ervin Laszlo. Thank you for your unwavering support. You have been instrumental in getting this book out into the world and my gratitude for you is inexpressible. You have been a gift to me and you are a gift to the world. You remain an ever-present defining influence for my work and you have been instrumental in my redefinition of my own vocational path, inspiring and encouraging me to found the WorldShift Movement as a dedication and abiding commitment to your own vision, contribution, and love for humanity and the Earth.

Barbara Marx Hubbard. Thank you for supporting me in my work and for the beautiful testimonial you wrote for this book. Your offering to humanity is a blessing to us all. You, along with Ervin Laszlo, are the pioneers in conscious evolution and I feel truly blessed to have the grace and gift of your validation of my own work. You are a divine blessing to us all and for the Earth.

Jude Currivan. Thank you for your encouragement, support, advice, and unwavering belief that this book would find a publisher. Your open heart and unconditional loving wisdom bestow such healing upon all those whose lives you touch and the Earth herself.

Professor Stephen Brown. Thank you for being the catalyst for the birth of this book through helping me to believe that I could write it and for your practical support in the initial editing process.

Jon Graham at Inner Traditions. Thank you for the deep respect, openness, and warmth you have shown me. A nature like yours in the commercial world is rare and I feel blessed to have been guided to you.

John Hays at Inner Traditions. Another special being who works for a special publisher. Thank you for the respect, consideration, and warmth you always show me.

Nancy Yeilding. My editor. Thank you for respecting the message and energy that permeates this book through your exquisitely sensitive editing.

Inner Traditions. My gratitude to all those whom I have come into contact with during this process. I am delighted and encouraged by the open-hearted respect and warmth that you all express. Inner Traditions is the ideal publisher for this book, as you have embodied new-paradigm values and elevated consciousness in all your dealings with me.

Geoff Stray, good friend and 2012 brother. Thank you for all of your guidance and advice when it came to the edits of 2012/Mayan/ astronomical facts in the early chapters of this book.

Cherry Williams, my dear, dear friend. Thank you for your unwavering and constant support, insights, and advice, much of which influenced the content of this book. Thank you for walking every step of the journey with me and for the commitment and devotion you showed when editing the manuscript with me.

Richard Spurgeon, soul brother. Thank you for the dedication you put into coediting and perfecting the final draft of the manuscript with me.

David Woolfson, dear friend, co-initiator and colleague at WorldShift Movement. Thank you for your devoted friendship, support, visionary nature, and unwavering belief in me. Your presence in my life has proven instrumental in this book being published.

Gifted oracles Donna White and Anna-Kaye. Thank you for your incredibly accurate psychic insights, which foretold my writing of this book before I ever had any idea about it. Your ongoing guidance has proven over and over to have been not only instrumental, but invaluable to this book now being in the world.

My beloved sister, Manuela Harrison. Thank you for lifetimes of sisterhood, friendship, and twinship. Thank you for your total love of and faith in who I am, my work, and this book.

Luke Owen, dear friend and soul brother. Thank you for unconditionally supporting me throughout the entire process of writing and editing this book. Thank you for making it possible for me to write or edit for up to sixteen hours a day, over five months, by taking care of my every need at a practical level. This made it possible for me to give myself entirely to the process of bringing this book to the world. You are the silent angel in the background that made it possible for me to write this book with the speed it required.

Ursula Athene, dear cherished friend. Thank you for unconditionally loving and supporting me and for believing in everything I do. Your presence in my life is a great blessing. You are the embodiment of unconditional love, toward everyone and every living creature, and are a shining mirror for me in my quest to continually cultivate the same.

Janice Haddon, dear, dear friend and soul sister. Thank you for your constant support, for your editing suggestions, for your humor and for your unconditionally loving presence.

Dana Amma Day, dear goddess friend and sister, co-initiator and colleague at WorldShift Movement, and CEO of Positive TV. Thank you for your positive belief in my work and for your unconditional loving support.

Violaine Corradi, a very special Earth Angel and dear sister. Thank you for all your support and for composing the beautiful music for the *Clarion Call* CDs. Your presence on this Earth is a gift for humanity and your presence in my life is a great gift for me.

Malcolm Wright, dear friend, co-initiator and colleague at WorldShift Movement. Thank you for your constant support, dependability, and grounded guidance with *Clarion Call*. Thank you for your giftedness and genius when it comes to all things related to the Internet and websites. The reassurance I experience because you are in my life is beyond value or words.

Marcus Mason. Dear friend. Thank you for your guidance and expertise with the astrological data and explanation of specific terminologies and for your reliability and support and love and humor!

Joyce Scott. My dearly loved mum. Thank you for your unconditional belief and love. I am so blessed to have had you in my life and so joyful at what great friends we have become over the years, which just gets more wonderful.

John Scott. My dear lovely brother. Thank you for your unconditional acceptance, love, and support of me and for my work.

Donie Quirke. Dear brother and friend. Thank you for your unwavering belief in me and for the unconditional support, emotionally and materially, that you have shown to me.

And finally . . .

For all those who have engaged in conversation with me in service of their own conscious evolution and self-healing. Thank you for the honor of inviting me to walk alongside you on your path of Self-discovery, which was also my own. As Lilla Watson so beautifully summarizes in a quote that may serve well anyone who reaches a hand out to support another: "If you have come to help me, you are wasting your time. But if you have come because your liberation is bound up with mine, then let us work together." To each of you I offer my eternal gratitude for the gift of liberation that journeying with you has bestowed upon me.

It is said that many Great Beings incarnate into the bodies of animals and come to bring us a special teaching in a unique way. The Indigenous Elders speak often of the spiritual significance of animals who are white in color, who hold an exceptionally fine vibration and bring Great Light for humanity. Their message to the world and to those they choose to come into contact with when incarnate is one of High Spiritual Teaching and Healing. Miracle the Sacred White Buffalo is but one example.

In my own life I have had the Divine Blessing to experience this ancient belief for myself.

A very special thank you goes to my beloved Kaunuk, a beautiful white German Shepherd who left this realm on November 24, 2010, aged just five and a half. It is Kaunuk who has proved to be my greatest Spiritual Teacher. His is the spirit of a Master and what he taught me during his brief stay on Earth has been singularly the most transformative and beautiful experience of my life. Kaunuk's message to us all is this: "Remember no matter how challenged we may feel by our lives, our bodies, or our circumstances, find a moment each day to play, laugh, and smile, for no other reason than that this is our true nature." We must always try to remember to stay connected to this reality, that we may express this truth, which so many of us have lost touch with.

Kaunuk reminds us "not to forget our humanity. To take time to be kind, caring, loving, and forgiving to each other, no matter how busy or tired we might be. To pause from whatever we are doing and reach out and touch, love, and connect with another, even in the midst of the ensuing whirlwind of the ever increasing demands of the times we live in."

Kaunuk wishes for us all to understand how Joy and Play are the sweet-tasting Medicine we need to transform our own lives and that can carry us across the threshold of the death of the old world and into the new.

My beloved Kaunuk, with all my heart I thank you.
I honor you. I love you.

9 March 2005 – 24 November 2010

Introduction

It has been said that our generation is the first in history that can decide whether it's the last in history. We need to add that our generation is also the first in history that can decide whether it will be the first generation of a new phase in history. We have reached a watershed in our social and cultural evolution.

ERVIN LASZLO,
TWICE NOBEL PEACE PRIZE NOMINEE
AND AUTHOR OF *WORLDSHIFT 2012*

December 21, 2012, is an extraordinary date in our calendar. It marks the precise moment when important ancient prophecies and rare astronomical alignments converge to mark the great *Shift of Ages*. Some of you may be familiar with the 2012 prophecies and may have read about the two possible outcomes as we reach this momentous moment in Earth's history. One of these speaks of the resurrection of the Earth and her inhabitants into what many of the ancient prophecies refer to as a "Golden Millennium," whereas other theories suggest we are heading for "Armageddon."

Although for some years I had a sense of the importance of the impending 2012 date, I had not considered weaving this into my own

1

work until April 2009, when I was "visited" by Miracle, the Sacred White Buffalo, who passed over in September 2004. Her birth had been foretold by a two-thousand-year-old prophecy of the Native American peoples known collectively as the Sioux.* They prophesied that the birth of a female white buffalo calf who would later change color four times would indicate that humankind was on the threshold of a thousand years of peace. Miracle appeared to me in a vision as clearly as if she was physically in the room. She telepathically conveyed to me a series of visions indicating the profound importance of the time leading up to 2012. She invited me to follow her guidance and I made a choice to do so in an instant. Her appearance catalyzed the alignment of my soul to its higher purpose and from that moment I have been on an incredible journey.

Miracle's energy became an almost permanent fixture and I was aware of her at all times. Simultaneously, the spiritual guides who work with me, whom I shall refer to as the "Luminous Ones," gathered closer to me and impressed upon my consciousness that I was being invited to write a book, record accompanying audio-therapy CDs, and work with groups of people to assist them in aligning with their higher purpose. The title *2012: A Clarion Call* was given to me and it was impressed upon me that the world needed a *call* to action and awareness. I was invited to be the channel for this message.

This is the book that you now hold in your hands. It includes channeled information from the Luminous Ones, highly advanced guides and masters who overlight humanity and work in service of human and planetary evolution. It contains what they wish to convey to the world at this critical point in human evolution. It is a union of the earthly and the heavenly, grounded in earthly wisdom and exalted by transformational channelings from the Spirit realms. This book is written *for the people.* This means that it has been written for all

---

*For more about Miracle and how this book came to be, please see appendix I.

people, from all walks of life. It is offered to *all* regardless of religious, spiritual, or philosophical beliefs, race or cultural background. It is less a *book* and more a *manual;* it is an invitation to *all.*

This book is intended to serve as a catalyst to awaken the consciousness and spirituality of those still "sleeping," to alert those who are partly awake, and to inform and inspire those who are already awakened. Read it not from your head but with your heart. *Feel* the energy of the words. The *Clarion Call* invites you to join me in a wonderful journey of self-discovery, self-healing, and self-actualization. It is my hope that it will motivate you to make a conscious choice to become an active co-creator who serves the Earth and the next evolutionary step for humanity. It is hoped that by reading *2012: A Clarion Call* you will come to understand the profound meaning of the times we live in and that your heightened awareness will support the shift of consciousness needed in the years approaching 2012. May the knowledge contained herein inspire you to embrace your soul's higher purpose, ensuring the manifestation of a new world.

While there is a plethora of information concerning 2012 available to us, via the Internet, books, articles, seminars, and so on, much of it is extremely complex and confusing and often written in a language that few really comprehend. This can unintentionally discourage even the most ardent of seekers who quite simply feel that they need an interpreter to understand the material. I have attempted to decipher much of the complexity of this information so that it reaches you in a simple, concise format. I have sought to extract the pure essence from the relevant and accurate reams of available information on matters pertaining to 2012.

The purpose behind sharing this information is for it to catalyze, accelerate, and raise your consciousness. *2012: A Clarion Call* is a call to those who sense an undeniable gnosis that something significant is happening on a global level. It is for those who feel a powerful urge to know and from that knowing feel empowered to respond to an inner and outer *call to action.* Through this book and its companion

CDs* I offer myself as your guide, that I may support you to discover your unique offering to the world. A higher-dimensional, powerfully transformative energy is woven into the pages of this book and the audio-therapy journeys; it permeates each word and will register on many levels of your conscious, unconscious, and superconscious mind.

This book offers you an opportunity to engage in some deep inner searching and invites you to explore exactly what your contribution might be as we move closer to the great change ahead, the Shift of Ages. As you journey deep into *2012: A Clarion Call,* I invite you to adopt an attitude of *interested curiosity* and allow yourself to become open and receptive when reading and contemplating what your own contribution might be. By remaining *curious* about your responses or reactions, you will begin to understand your reasons for choosing to be here on the Earth at this time. This book offers you a promise, that in knowing and aligning with your unique role as we approach 2012, you will never have felt more alive, purposeful, or connected with yourself and to both the heavenly and earthly realms.

You will find a glossary of special terms at the back of the book along with a resource directory with a list of contacts and organizations that may further assist you in the evolution of your consciousness. Two appendices are also provided. Appendix I, as mentioned, elaborates upon the story of Miracle, the Sacred White Buffalo, and her role in the birthing of this book. Appendix II details some of the methods and practices that are of particular benefit in healing the traumas that interfere with our ability to know our own vastness and to live our greater purpose.

---

*2012: A Clarion Call has three companion CDs, each containing three channeled healing journeys, supporting deep personal process work for transformation. These audio-therapy CDs encourage you to participate with what you read and have the potential to transform not only your mind, but also your energy field, which is the source of self-actualization. They are available at www.nicolyachristi.com. I suggest that you wait until you have finished reading this book before you engage in the audio-therapy exercises, as the book serves to prepare the ground for the transformational experiences that the CDs can catalyze.

The journey you are about to embark upon could prove to be one that is both catalytic and enlightening. Reading this book can change your life. May it serve to support you in the rediscovery of your own unique contribution to humanity leading up to and beyond 2012. May all that you find here prove to motivate, inspire, and transform your perceptions of yourself, others, the world, and the universe, and may it provide you with exactly what you need during these pivotal times.

Now let the journey begin.

CHAPTER ONE

Who Were the Maya and Why Is 2012 So Important?

Here at the end of an age we finally have an opportunity to discover not only what we have done but who we really are.

SHARRON ROSE, *TIMEWAVE 2012/2013*

The Maya represent one of the great civilizations on Earth. For millennia they were residents of the Yucatan Peninsula, Guatemala, Belize, some parts of Mexico, El Salvador, and Honduras. Evidence of this great culture is found scattered across Yucatan jungles and in the highlands of present-day Guatemala, where the remnants of ancient cities and temple sites are to be found, in addition to intricately designed plazas, towering stepped pyramids, and centers of ceremony and worship, which are adorned with the finest sculpted stones and covered in hieroglyphic inscriptions.

During the period in Mayan history known as the Pre-Classic era (2000 BCE to 250 CE), the Maya developed a farming culture. This was also the period when the astonishing structures were built in Mesoamerica, including those at sites such as Copan, Palenque, Chich'en Itza, and the palace of Xpuhil. Many Mayan temples are said

6

to represent gateways containing sacred knowledge, which allow the cosmos, the Earth, and humanity to integrate and unite. There are also moments in the Mayan time cycles that are said to represent gateways.

The Maya were an astronomically and cosmically advanced civilization believed to be in direct contact with galactic energy and specifically with Pleiadians (fifth-dimensional beings from the Pleiades star system who are far more advanced than humanity) during the Classic Maya period. This explains the mystery of how the Maya knew of the 400 stars in the Pleiades, when today we see only seven with the naked eye. With all our modern technology and resources we are still unable to measure astronomical data more accurately. According to contemporary Mayan Daykeeper,* Hunbatz Men, the Maya believe that the Milky Way is the generator of all life. Author Jose Argüelles says that the stars serve as lenses that transmit energies to planets and that our Sun is the lens through which galactic energies are transmitted as light codes to the Earth.

During the peak period known as the Classic Maya civilization, approximately 435–830 CE, they were ruled for sixty-eight years (615–683 CE) by one known as Lord Pacal. He ruled over the city of Palenque and its empire, situated in today's state of Chiapas, Mexico. It is said that Pacal came to illuminate the Mayan people and was an enlightened being. His mission on Earth was to guide the Mayan people toward the light of cosmic wisdom, thus allowing human beings to attain enlightenment (liberation from the restrictions of the third dimension, the physical world anchored in a linear time- and space-based reality where human consciousness resides) and complete our destiny. Pacal was said to be a great initiate, capable of miraculous healings simply by raising his hand or with just a glance. He was said to be a master of energy, which he could control with his body and mind.

Pacal was known as a magician of time. He had an intricate understanding of the complexity of numbers and mathematics, interpreting

---

*Daykeepers were the masters of the ancient stone altars found in sacred places throughout the world, from Stonehenge to Machu Picchu. A Daykeeper is able to call on the power of these ancient altars to heal and bring balance to the world.

these as a language that transcends human verbal expression. Pacal taught his people about the thirteen dimensions that hold the explanation of all mysteries, the thirteen realms in which physical or energetic realities manifest in ascending frequencies. One of his messages was that "God is a number," illustrating the Mayan belief that we are intimately connected with and influenced by the galaxy. Pacal's knowledge of great cycles of time allowed him to record this information for future humanity. He is renowned for guiding the inscription of stone monuments with precise astronomical and astrological information, which was part of the Mayan mission. He knew that as a species humanity would become ignorant of the sacred connection to nature and become disconnected from the laws of the natural world.

The ancient Maya were responsible for the most complex calendar system in the world. They derived more than seventeen calendars, using a unique and exceptionally simple calculation system to create calendars for equinoxes, solstices, and eclipse cycles as well as the synchronization of the cycles of Mercury. Only one of these seventeen calendars, known as the "Long Count calendar," preoccupies modern day humans. The origins or pioneers of this calendar are not known. Evidence suggests that the Maya inherited the Long Count calendar from an even more ancient people of Central America, most likely the Olmec. This calendar began on 11–08–3114 BCE and is set to complete at the winter solstice of 2012, an era of 5,125.26 years. In addition to adopting and radically advancing the existing calendar systems from earlier cultures, taking astronomical understanding to an extraordinarily high level, the Maya also applied their highly advanced technological abilities and wisdom to the arts, where they created some of the most amazing carvings known to the world. Their working of hard volcanic stone and gems was outstanding. They would bore holes into tiny jade beads that were so precise that today we would need to use our most advanced technologies to match them.

The collapse of the Classic Maya occurred around 900 CE, when almost an entire civilization literally disappeared over a hundred-year period. There has been much speculation as to why this occurred and how this could have happened. Mayan experts have researched the possibilities of drought, pestilence, and internal feuding to find explanations of what may have led to their disappearance. Some theories suggest that they simply abandoned their lands, dispersing throughout the globe, setting up new indigenous cultures, including Native American tribes like the Hopi. No proof of these or any other theories has come to light.

Others speak of the Mayan civilization of that time "ascending," that is, literally ascending from the Earth over a period of one hundred years, returning to their cosmic origins in the Pleiades. Not all of the Maya left, yet it was not until the tenth century that the Mayan civilization re-emerged. This new Mayan culture became known as the "New Empire Maya." What is clear is that approximately nine million people disappeared during the course of a century. What will almost certainly remain a mystery is why and where.

Although most of the sacred codices of the Maya were destroyed by the Spanish missionaries, some were preserved. It has taken three generations of scholars to decipher them, allowing us access to some of the primary codes that constitute their cosmic knowledge. The Maya speak of "Five Worlds" or "Suns," each lasting 13 baktuns or 5,125 years. All five equate to 26,000 years, the time it takes for the completion of a "Grand Cycle" (precession of the equinoxes). The reason that the cycles of the Mayan calendars are so relevant to us, thousands of years later, is because these systems describe an end point of December 21, 2012. The Maya used stone carvings to preserve the calendar that encodes the vital end date of Earth's current 26,000 year evolutionary cycle. It seems they knew that this moment in evolution would prove to be a critical and transformative period, as by this point humanity would be far from living harmoniously with the laws of nature. This information was recorded for posterity as a warning to help us avert further catastrophes.

The mission of the Classic Maya appears to have been to synchronize the solar system, the Earth, and its future inhabitants with the much larger galactic community. The ways of the Maya became lost as we descended into a dark age. But now their ancient and profound wisdom has remerged at a critical time to guide and reconnect us back to Oneness at a personal, collective, galactic, universal, and cosmic level.

The winter solstice of 2012 is a grand alignment where many cycles within cycles converge and merge within one moment in time. In the West, we know only of "linear" time, which consists of past and future, cause and effect. Indigenous and shamanic cultures perceived time to be cyclical; rather than travelling in a straight line, it turned like a wheel. The chakras or energy centers found in the human energy system are a mirror of this. These cycles of time are based on synchronicity and enable us to influence past situations, as well as tap into future destiny. What is interesting is what this illustrates about many of our modern-day healing modalities, which point to past events as causing current day maladies. With cyclical time we can revisit our past and our future (note the term *revisit:* according to indigenous cultures, our future, present, and past lives are lived concurrently). This releases us from the belief that we are a result of our genetics, conditioning, or karma (the sum of all our individual experiences, past, present, and future).

We now have an opportunity to reconnect to ancient wisdom in the years leading to 2012, in ways that I will reveal later in the book. We can evolve beyond linear time and enter into cyclical time, allowing us to reach into the past, present, and future simultaneously to repair, regenerate, and rebalance. Human-made linear time has set us apart from nature. It is imperative that we learn to harmonize with the rhythm of the living universe.

THE GOLDEN AGE

Men were neither bought nor sold; there were no poor and no rich; there was no need to labor, because all that men required was obtained by the power of will; the chief virtue was the abandonment of all worldly desires. There was no disease; there was no lessening with the years; there was no hatred or vanity, or evil thought whatsoever; no sorrow, no fear. All mankind could attain to supreme blessedness.

MAHABHARATA

In the Mayan spiritual belief system the end of a world age is a time of great opportunity. Each time this occurs humanity can choose to move into a new, more harmonious age or face an apocalyptic catastrophe. The evidence shows that many modern indigenous peoples of the Americas, most notably the Hopi but also other tribes—from the furthest regions of the Amazon jungles in the South, to the frozen wastes of the Canadian North—agree with the Maya. In their mythology the Aztecs have recorded the dates of four catastrophic events when humanity was largely obliterated by floods, fire, wind, and earthquakes. Pacal spoke of the closing of this world age cycle on 21 December 2012, which is the also the date the Maya foretell as being the *beginning of a new creation.* As we approach the world of the sixth sun beginning in 2012, we are also in the last three years of the 26,000-year completion cycle, which heralds the beginning of what the Maya and the Incas have prophesied to be a "Golden Age."

The term *Golden Age* is found in many ancient cultures, including those of the Hopi and the Greek, who also speak of three additional ages, the Silver, Bronze, and the Iron (also known as the Dark Age). The most ideal of these was the Golden Age when humankind was pure and immortal and lived in harmony. The Vedic or ancient Hindu culture saw history as being cyclical and composed of *yugas,* or "ages," with alternating dark and golden ages. The Kali Yuga (Iron Age), Dwapara Yuga (Bronze Age), Treta Yuga (Silver Age), and Satya Yuga (Golden Age) correspond to the four Greek races. The Greek poet Hesiod was the first to describe previous races or generations of people, the earliest being the Golden race, who lived in an idyllic age. This race was succeeded by progressively inferior races, those of the Silver, Bronze and Iron, the latter referring to present-day humanity.

Four Ages in the History of Humanity

The Golden Age: This was the first age of the world, an untroubled and prosperous era during which people lived in ideal happiness. It is the age when we had our greatest connection to Source (the very Beingness of God), an era when meditation, wisdom, and communion with Spirit held special importance. In the Satya Yuga the average life expectancy of a human being was believed to be about 400 years. This is an era when people practiced only loving-kindness and humankind lived in harmony with the earth.

The Silver Age: The point at which darkness entered human consciousness and we became separated from Spirit.

The Bronze Age: A greater spiritual darkness descended upon humanity with even further disconnection from Spirit.

The Iron Age/The Dark Age: In this age darkness has completely diminished the spiritual light and this is where we are now. However, we are on the point of entering a new age, another Golden Age.

It is important to understand that the Maya were interested in the period of time surrounding 21 December 2012, as well as that specific day. They point to a process known as "galactic alignment," which occurs when the winter solstice Sun exactly aligns with the position in the sky where the ecliptic plane (the Sun's apparent path) intersects the galactic equator of the Milky Way, forming a "cosmic cross." This thirty-six-year process began in 1980 and will end in 2016. It marks the point in the four ages at which we reach the greatest degree of separation between matter and spirit, otherwise referred to as "galactic midnight."

Many past civilizations considered the 21 December 2012 date to be of great importance, including ancient people from the Americas, Sumer, China, and Egypt. In Egypt, the pyramids of the Giza plateau appear to provide both a time marker and an optimum viewing platform for the astronomical phenomena associated with the winter solstice of 2012. The Qu'ero, direct descendents of the Incas, talk of "an age of conquest and domination coming to an end and a new human being born." They talk of Earth being restored to its former beauty and grace. They call this process the "Turning of the Earth" and they identify 2012 as the time when this unfolds.

We now have a once-in-a-26,000-year opportunity to bypass the painstaking and lengthy process involved in moving through each preceding age to return to the Golden Age. By a divine act of grace, we can simply step out of the dark age in which we are still immersed, and move into the light of a new age, a golden age. However, this will require some degree of courage and vision.

The world will not end. It will be transformed. . . . Everything will change. . . . Change is accelerating now and it will continue to accelerate. If the people of the Earth can get to this 2012 date without having destroyed too much of the Earth, we will rise to a new, higher level. But to get there we must transform enormously powerful forces that seek to block the way. Humanity will continue, but in a different way. Material structures will change. From this we will have the opportunity to be more human. Our planet can be renewed or ravaged. Now is the time to awaken and take action. The prophesized changes are going to happen, but our attitude and actions determine how harsh or mild they are.

This is a crucially important moment for humanity and for Earth. Each person is important. If you have incarnated into this era, you have spiritual work to do balancing the planet. The greatest wisdom is in simplicity. Love, respect, tolerance, sharing, gratitude, forgiveness. It's not complex or elaborate. The real knowledge is free. It's encoded in your DNA. All you need is within you. Great teachers have said that from the beginning. Find your heart, and you will find your way.

MAYAN MESSENGER CARLOS BARRIOS

CHAPTER TWO

2012: The Shift of Ages

People feel instinctively the impetus from the Earth herself to wake up and make a difference.

JEAN HOUSTON

Never before in the history of humankind has your contribution to the world been more needed. Never before in our history could your contribution make the difference between humanity stepping onto a new path of light, or remaining on the existing path of destruction, as we step over the much-prophesied threshold of 2012.

To put it simply, there are two options ahead of us, as predicted by ancient civilizations. One option is to continue on the current dysfunctional path that ultimately leads to destruction. The second is to step onto a new path that will lead us to a new Earth and a new way forward that ensures not only the survival but the flourishing of the Earth and all life. Which of these two paths do you choose? One is the way of love, light, consciousness, truth, liberation, unity, and transformation. The other is a path of fear, suffering, darkness, unconsciousness, manipulation, conditioning, and duality. The choice is ours. We can either choose the path of love or the path of fear. Each individual decision is now critical to the outcome.

The Clarion Call is a call to those who are aware of the coming 2012 threshold, as well as to those who are not. This is a call to ALL, regardless of age, nationality, religious, spiritual, philosophical, or educational background. Many thousands of us are now needed to unify in order to ensure that humanity takes the next evolutionary step. If we are unable to raise personal and planetary consciousness we may not succeed in crossing the 2012 threshold into what the Tibetans and Q'ero (the modern day Incas) refer to as a "Golden Age of Peace." We need to unite and dedicate ourselves to work for the highest good of the collective.

We are being supported in this quest by legions of multidimensional beings who overlight the Earth plane. They are urging us to become vigilant and prepare to redefine our individual roles in these next few years, so that we may help to birth a new world consciousness. Our individual and collective task, supported by these great beings of light in the higher dimensions, is to assist in the coming transition from third-dimensional consciousness to fifth-dimensional consciousness. The fifth dimension is the higher dimension where our light-body—our energy body that connects us with the universal mind—resides.

To gain some perspective of the enormity and meaning of the times we live in, take a look at the following astronomical and astrological events and cosmological theories:

- The Western astrological system speaks of the Shifts of Ages, when one great astrological age moves into another. We are currently moving from the Age of Pisces into the Age of Aquarius.
- It is believed that we are now at the completion point of a multimillion year circular orbit of our galaxy around the great central Sun at the center. (One orbit of the galaxy takes 225–250 million years; it is believed to have completed between 20–25 orbits since it first formed.) Our galaxy moves through space in the form of continuous connecting circles, like a great cosmic spiral. As it completes this multimillion-year orbit, our galaxy is connecting diagonally to the next ring in the cosmic spiral. When this happens, all of the planets, solar systems, and their inhabitants

simultaneously take an initiatory step into a new evolutionary cycle.

- We are at the end of a 26,000-year cycle of Earth, Sun, and galactic plane (the plane in which the majority of a disk-shaped galaxy's mass lies). From our perspective on Earth, the December solstice sun moves across the galactic plane—an event that occurs once every 26,000 years—the result of which is to attune consciousness to higher frequencies (imagine shifting focus from lower to higher chakras).

- We are in the last two years of a 5,125-year Mayan creation cycle.

- The winter solstice of 1998 was the midway point of the thirty-six-year galactic alignment process. Because the Sun is so large (about half a degree wide), it will not complete its journey across the galactic equator until 2016. This process is predicted to induce extraordinary transformations in human consciousness.

- The coming end date of December 21, 2012, is written as 13.0.0.0.0 in Mayan Long Count notation. It is the end of the current era and the start of the next era of the Long Count calendar. The start of the current era in 3114 BCE is also written as 13.0.0.0.0. In Mayan time philosophy, the end is also the beginning of the next cycle, though some people refer to 22 December 2012 as the first day of the next cycle, because it is 0.0.0.0.1.

- On December 21, 2012, Jupiter, Pluto, and Saturn will be involved in an astrological formation known as a Yod (finger of God). This translates to a higher vision (Jupiter) being projected out onto the physical plane (Saturn) and permeating spiritual will (Pluto). It allows us an opportunity to align our spiritual and physical will, and wholly supports us in the manifestation of a higher vision, while at the same time letting go of the old (Jupiter retrograde). This ties into the completion process suggested by the events of 21 December 2012.

- 2012 marks the completion of a profoundly important phase of global healing that accelerated in 1999 at the time of the solar eclipse. The Maya describe this period of thirteen years as "the Quickening."

So December 21, 2012, is a very significant date. Each year the December solstice sun aligns with the equator midline of the Milky Way. To gain a perspective on this, imagine the Earth's equator, which forms the division between the northern and southern hemispheres. Astronomically, the winter solstice sun has been pointing into the southern galactic hemisphere for 13,000 years. As we approach perfect alignment with the galactic equator, a thirty-six year process will conclude, at which point the winter solstice Sun will have been reoriented to point to the northern galactic hemisphere.

The widest part of the Milky Way is known as the "dark rift," which corresponds to the direction of the center of the galaxy. John Major Jenkins, researcher of Mayan cosmology and philosophy, and author of the books, *Maya Cosmogenesis 2012, Galactic Alignment,* and *The 2012 Story,* tells us that as the 2012 winter solstice Sun aligns with the dark rift and the solstice meridian then passes to the other side of the center of the galactic equator, this will create a *field effect energy reversal.* As we resonate with the field sourced from the galactic center, we will be affected by this changing orientation. The end of the Mayan Long Count calendar will culminate in a pole shift in our collective consciousness.

The final activations of 2012 are:

- On June 6, 2012, Venus will transit the Sun, that is, it will travel between the Sun and the Earth. Venus transits come in pairs every eight years. The first of the current Venus transits occurred on June 8, 2004, and the next occurs on June 6, 2012, after which it will not occur again until 2117. Ancient calendar scholars tell that the 2012 transit will be a rare and very special conjunction of the Sun and Venus; it is said that a new world consciousness will be born during it. It is believed that the Maya understood that a Venus transit acted like a "circuit breaker," switching off the sunspot cycle and impacting the Sun, Moon, Earth, and Venus system. Every planet has its own unique frequency or rate of vibration; since ancient times, Venus has been connected with divine, unconditional love. During a transit, the Sun's rays amplify and direct the frequency of Venus toward the Earth, bathing it in the energies of Venus for seven hours.

- Venus is getting closer to aligning with the Pleiades and will conjunct Alcyone, the star of the Pleiades, on April 3, 2012. Some believe that Alcyone now holds Earth's Akashic Records (information of our past, present, and future lives).

- On May 20, 2012, there will be a rare solar eclipse in which the Sun and Moon conjunct the Pleiades.

- A second solar eclipse on November 13, 2012, will occur close to the Serpens, the serpent held by Ophiuchus, found in the thirteenth constellation, situated between Scorpio and Sagittarius. Ophiuchus is also known as the shaman/serpent healer.*

In 1999, according to Mayan cosmology, we entered the last of thirteen thirteen-year cycles. The Maya prophesied the start of this phase as the solar eclipse of 1999, which they said would coincide with an unprecedented planetary alignment known as a "grand cross," consisting of the fixed signs of the zodiac known as Leo, Taurus, Scorpio, and Aquarius. Two thousand years before this significant cosmic occurrence, the Bible prophesied "An angel with four faces, one of a bull, one of an eagle, one of a man, and one of a lion."

The Maya foretold that these final thirteen years of the 5,125-year calendar would be the last opportunity for our civilization to embrace the changes that are due to unfold at the moment of our collective spiritual regeneration in December 2012. They prophesied that in the final thirteen-year cycle, humanity would have just thirteen years left to transform our consciousness and raise our vibration. They foretold that seven years after entering that thirteen-year phase (2006), we would enter a time of darkness in which we would be forced to confront our

---

*For much more detailed information about these and other significant 2012 astronomical events and Mayan cosmology, see Geoff Stray's book, *Beyond 2012* (Rochester, Vt.: Bear and Company, 2009) and website: www.diagnosis2012.co.uk.

actions. They talk of humankind entering "The Sacred Hall of Mirrors" where we need to look at ourselves and consider our conduct toward each other and the planet.

Let us also note that the Earth's kundalini has recently realigned. Kundalini is the most powerful energy within the human body. Known as the "serpent energy," it is located at the base of the spine. Kundalini generally remains dormant unless activated by spiritual practice; then, when it is awakened, it catalyzes profound transformations within the consciousness and the energetic system of an individual. In his book, *Serpent of Light,* consciousness transformer Drunvalo Melchizedek, speaks of the Earth as also having kundalini energy, which, unlike that of most humans, is active. He explains how this energy remains attached to one location for a 13,000-year period, after which it relocates to another, where it will remain for another 13,000 years. These 13,000 years are based upon the precession of the equinoxes.* When this serpent energy moves, it is said to transform humanity's perception and expression of spirituality.

Drunvalo mentions that the Earth's kundalini has two poles: one at the exact center of the Earth and the other located at a specific point on the Earth's surface. There is a pulse of 12,920 years, at which point the poles reverse. The Earth's consciousness simultaneously shifts the location of the kundalini to a new location on the Earth's surface. According to Drunvalo, the surface location of the Earth's kundalini for the past 13,000 years has been Tibet. The process of the relocating of the serpent energy began in 1949 and it now resides in the Chilean Andes Mountains, in South America. In *Spontaneous Evolution* by

---

*According to Wikipedia, *precession* is "a change in the orientation of the rotation axis of a rotating body. In astronomy, axial precession is a gravity-induced, slow and continuous change in the orientation of an astronomical body's rotational axis. In particular, it refers to the gradual shift in the orientation of Earth's axis of rotation, which, like a wobbling top, traces out a cone in a cycle of approximately 26,000 years (called a Great or Platonic year in astrology). Earth's precession was historically called *precession of the equinoxes* because the equinoxes moved westward along the ecliptic relative to the fixed stars, opposite the motion of the Sun along the ecliptic."

Bruce Lipton and Steve Bhaerman (London: Hay House, 2009) they say: "The Dalai Lama has also spoken of it. He says he will be the last Dalai Lama from the Himalayas, and the next one will likely be from the other high mountains, the Andes."

Nobody knows what is to unfold post 2012, not even the Maya, Hopi, or other indigenous elders of our time. All that they can tell us is that this ending of a cycle is significant. Prophecy does not say what is going to happen beyond the 2012 date. Our fate and the Earth's destiny is in our hands. We have an extraordinary opportunity to unite as one heart in unity consciousness. If we do not unite but instead continue in duality consciousness, then we can expect nothing more than the continuation of our current situation of destruction and chaos.

The reality is that we have a one-way ticket to disaster unless we transform the way in which we treat the Earth and each other. The relationship we have with the Earth reflects the relationship we have with ourselves. How we treat ourselves and each other emotionally, mentally, and physically also has an impact on the Earth. We need only to look around us to understand the current state of human consciousness. There are places of extraordinary beauty on the Earth and there are places that have been damaged, distorted, and destroyed. When we look at the overall state of the Earth, we are looking into a mirror. There are places of immense beauty within each one of us and there are also places of dysfunction and distortion in most, which we project into the world. For the Earth to heal, we must heal.

Unity consciousness will unite us collectively in Oneness. We *can* create a world in which we respect each other, nature, the planet, all living energies, and sentient beings. We have a spiritual responsibility to protect the world for future generations, as well as the four-legged, two-legged, the winged, the bees, the butterflies, the aquatics, grasses, trees, flowers, mountains, and oceans. If we can unite in the spirit of unconditional love and equality we will fulfill the ancient prophecies that inform us that 2012 can lead us into a new and golden age.

CHAPTER THREE

Your Role in the Shift of Ages

We are praying, many of the medicine people, the spiritual leaders, the elders, are praying for the world. We are praying that mankind does wake up and think about the future, for we haven't just inherited this Earth from our ancestors, but we are borrowing it from our unborn children.

JOSEPH CHASING-HORSE

Indigenous elders, including the Maya, have sent out a specific message to the world, a warning to humanity that we *have* to change the way we live and how we treat the planet. For every prophecy about 2012 that speaks of transition and transformation there is one that talks of destruction and apocalypse. It is now imperative that we unite to support the Earth and each other, so that both may be strong enough to avert the possible catastrophes. It is essential to listen to *all* of the information available to us regarding the potential outcome for humanity from 2012. We cannot simply choose to align with the prophecy that requires the least action from us. It is irresponsible on our parts to remain uninformed, or to be informed and then not to take action or remain unconcerned about the outcome. Will we experience an era of

21

peace or the destruction of the Earth? Both are possible outcomes. We have a human responsibility to contribute if we are to manifest a prophecy that foretells of "a thousand years of peace."

Collectively, as communities and as individuals, we are no longer able to continue in the same way. To believe there is nothing that can be done will lead us to the ultimate destruction. We must become empowered, each and every one of us. We must take drastic and immediate action if we are to avoid the catastrophes warned of by various prophecies, including those of Nostradamus. Complacency is our greatest stumbling block and we cannot afford to be lazy or ignorant, as our attitude and actions will determine either a positive or negative outcome. Prophecies that foretell of a golden millennium are speaking of a *potential* outcome, one to be manifested by our taking action, reclaiming our power, raising our consciousness, and altering the collective vibration.

Now is the time to take the reins of our human and planetary destiny. The moment has come for us to be in the driving seat, directing the course of our future, instead of being taken for a ride by those whom *we have allowed* to take control of our destination. The decision makers who hold power in society and on a global scale need to gently and nonviolently be led away from the path of destruction they have us set upon. We need to establish a new way forward, one that serves the higher good of all. It is critical that we listen to, take heed and *act* upon the wisdom of ancient prophecies that speak of these transformative times.

It is now imperative that we understand the full scale of what lies ahead. We cannot dismiss apocalyptic prophecies as sensationalism. We do so at our peril. To be informed of all potential eventualities is a prerequisite for steering ourselves away from the current path of destruction and into a new world paradigm. How will we make a successful transition into a balanced new world if we sit back waiting to see what will unfold? Each day, as we approach 2012, we are making choices to live in darkness or move into the light. Make no mistake—we cannot remain inactive and hope that these predictions of catastrophe will not occur.

Take a look around you and witness the alarming decline of the pollinating species. What is it going to take for us as a collective to say "Enough!" and to take action to create a better world for ourselves and all life on the Earth? If the bee population continues to decline, (the cause of which is believed to come down to human tampering with nature) we will see the end of many flowers, fruits, and vegetables. We will live in a world with few natural colors, perfumes, or flavors. We have become separated from ourselves, each other, and Mother Nature. Will you continue to allow fellow humans to suffer, the abuse of animals including those hunted to extinction, the manipulation and abuse of nature, and the destruction of the Earth?

Our compliance with and acceptance of the current world system reduces us to mere cogs in a machine, driven by the agendas of global business structures, the media, government, consumer, and industrial powers. Our passive acceptance is what keeps this machine going. We need to recognize that we support the continuation of a dysfunctional global system when we sit back and expect a better future to manifest of its own accord, or believe that a handful of global activists can make this possible. We must all become global activists. An architect can hand you the design and building plans for a beautiful house that could be yours if you were willing to build it. However without your input the house will not build itself.

From 2013 onward, for the first time in human history we find ourselves without prophecy that offers details, other than indicating a transition into a golden age. In effect, we have a blank slate upon which to write a new story for humanity. 2013 calls on us to live in the Now, with what is, and to create our future in the moment. However, we need to make possible the potential of 2013 by ensuring a successful transition over the 2012 threshold. If we can set aside our personal differences and unite to focus our efforts on raising consciousness, this will ensure the golden future for all life spoken of by many 2012 prophecies.

Why do you imagine that ancient prophecies do not extend past 2012, other than to suggest to humanity that we have an opportunity to live in an era of great peace and harmony? Could it be that those ancient wise ones simply did not know if we would rise or fall at the time of the Shift of Ages? Much of ancient prophecy speaks of a "transformation of human consciousness." The old-world paradigm "victim" mentality has convinced us that "S**t Happens." However, the new-world mantra is "Shift Happens," and it most certainly will if we actively engage in the coming transition. By having a positive intent, we *can* manifest the promising outcome of a harmonious new-world paradigm. There is an increasing urgency for each of us to identify and transcend what stands between us and our contribution to the co-creation of a peaceful, just, and sustainable world.

YOUR SOUL'S PURPOSE AND PLANETARY REBIRTH

Humanity is about to cross a threshold, one that takes us from an old paradigm into a new one. It is now vital that we move to *the next level* of consciousness so our presence here, at this critical time in history, aids the ascension* of humanity and the Earth. However you lead your life up to 2012 and whatever you choose to do following, it is vital that you now become conscious of your soul's higher purpose. You will be aided in doing so by having a clear understanding of what I mean when I use the term *soul* as well as the terms *small (or lower or conscious) self*, *higher Self*, and *Spirit*. Our *lower or small self* is our third-dimensional ego self or personality, our conscious self, living in the physical world of duality. It is enveloped within the aura or luminous energy field and identified with the physical body. The aura is generated from the light-body, an expansive body of light that extends outward beyond the aura,

---

Ascension is when the physical and energetic bodies reach higher dimensions without going through the death process, or when the cells of the physical body increase their vibration and can no longer remain in a physical state. This and other specialized terms found in this book are also defined in the glossary provided at the end.

sometimes for miles. I perceive that we are *Spirit*; it is at our core and it exists *beyond* the light-body. *Soul* is our immortal aspect. Our *higher Self* lives in a higher dimension and is the link between our conscious self and our soul. The higher Self can influence the lower self.

We can visualize this as a sequence of "bridges." The first is the most elevated bridge of Spirit, which connects to the bridge of the soul, which in turn is connected to the bridge of the higher Self, which acts as a highway to the lower self through the luminous energy field. None of these are separate; they are all interlinked.

The clearer the aura or luminous energy field, the more the influence of the soul is increased. Then the higher Self is able to anchor more fully into the aura, which in turn raises the vibration of the luminous energy field. At the same time, a higher vibrating luminous energy field allows for the soul to become more anchored and present. As the soul becomes more awakened, this in turn further activates the light-body; it is at this point that we are able to perceive the vastness of the Spirit, the vastness of who we are, and how our consciousness expands beyond the light-body into infinity. This is where the fullness of our Spirit and multidimensionality expresses beyond any comprehension that we may grasp at our current stage of soul development and evolution.

A part of us *knows,* and has always known, that beyond our personal world lies a greater purpose. We each have incarnated with a soul mission, although most people never remember it, as they are stuck in dysfunctional patterns that often originate from difficult and painful early childhood experiences and unresolved karma. However, many of us *are* beginning to remember, due to the various spiritual, psychotherapeutic, and healing self-exploration processes we have undertaken. If we use the analogy of an onion, many of us have spent years committed to peeling back the layers to re-encounter our true Self, which had been buried under years of history and conditioning. It is when we finally reach this core Self that we fully *remember.*

It is possible to express our gifts in the world proactively without the painstaking *peeling away of layers.* Accomplished artists, philosophers, musicians, poets, pioneers, inventors, healers, mediums, and great spiritual teachers have contributed enormously to the world. This is because of their ability to either bypass or utilize their emotional wounding to tap into their higher purpose. Such contributions have been vital in ensuring that we move forward on our collective evolutionary journey.

However, many of the great minds, creators, and sensitives of this world, such as musicians like Mozart or artists like van Gogh, writers like Tolstoy, pioneers like Howard Hughes, and humanitarians like Oskar Schindler, live unfulfilled personal lives, having psychologically split from their shadow, which then sabotages their lives at a personal level. They fail to develop any deep personal connection with themselves or with those around them. Unless such people seek to heal their personal wounds and trauma, deep inner fulfillment will remain out of reach to them. Fulfillment, not to be mistaken for security, arises from the integration of our personal and worldly lives as we heal ourselves, and in so doing we enhance the world in which we live.

Most of us forget our worldly mission and the gifts we incarnate with remain unexpressed. When we lose touch with our true Self, we are left with a sense of deep discontent and a marked lack of fulfillment. This inner vacuum causes many to find solace in religion, consumerism (the new religion), addictions, an unhealthy preoccupation with the news, media, and politics, sex, or anything that will fill that void. This inner void develops in early childhood when we may be ignored, humiliated, or shamed for attempting to express our individuality, raw talent, and uniqueness, expressions of our own creator spirit, which is but a reflection of the Divine Creator Spirit. We need to fully express our creative energy (each one of us is creative in our own way) and connect to our higher purpose so that we can enhance the world we live in.

Reclaiming our authentic selves will create a significant transformation of the world. We have lost touch with the heart of living—that is to say living from our hearts. Barack Obama reminds us that "We are the change" and "Yes we can!" Our personal mission is to BECOME who we truly are, to emerge from the chrysalis, as butterflies. We can reclaim the lost Self. We can help and support each other to remember our unique individuality as *creators* and by doing so, we *can* create a new world. Embodying our unique, impassioned, empowered, glorious true Self is our contribution to the world.

Gandhi said, "The truth is the truth even in a minority of one." We must stand in our truth, even if we are a lone voice in the vast crowd. Instead of investing our time, energy, and resources in filling the insatiable void within, we need to realize that it is never too late to rediscover ourselves. In order to do this we must recognize that we are not victims and that our suffering is largely of our own making. Gandhi was an exceptional role model of passive resistance, who showed us that we can create change through peaceful action. There are organizations and resources in our local communities and neighboring towns and cities that can support us in empowering ourselves to seek to transform the current global system, a system that has now served its purpose and needs to make way for a new, functional global system. We need only type "WorldShift 2012" into a search engine to be in touch with a group of like minds. We are not alone.

For those of you who believe you are too wounded, angry, sad, or unworthy, not intelligent or spiritual enough to align with your purpose, recognize that this is a myth you have been steeped in, for too long. We live in times that invite us to *let go* of the past, in a way that is not about repression, splitting off, or denial, but is about openness, integration, and balance. You can *choose* to release painful memories and experiences with the support of the incredible and effective healing tools that are now available. (Some of these are presented in appendix II and a comprehensive list of resources is provided at the end of the book.)

We are living in a high energy time wave that gifts us with many therapeutic processes that support us in letting go of the past and stepping into the new. Why hold onto pain when you can live in joy? It is as simple as a matter of choice—love or fear? Light or dark? It is up to you what life experience you choose. You always have a choice. Why hide in the shadows of your wounded self when you can step into the radiant light of your higher Self? We tend to hold fears, hurts, and resistances close to us like semiprecious jewels, afraid to let them go because we have built a whole identity and character around them. We have forgotten who we truly are. We have allowed ourselves to remain victims. However, if we seek to reclaim our authentic selves and refuse to let the past dictate our present and future lives, we will go from strength to strength and our lives will be forever transformed.

Letting go of the old and daring to step into the new will allow you to experience the beauty of your soul, and, perhaps for the first time in this life, come to know what peace and fulfillment truly are.

CHAPTER FOUR

Shifting Frequencies and the Ascension Process

Everything is frequency, and it only takes a little shift in frequency to affect all other frequencies. As frequency beings, you are to become aware, to transmute and expand, and to enter into the home of Spirit as people who lead people to lead themselves.

THE PLEIADIANS, THROUGH BARBARA MARCINIAK,
FAMILY OF LIGHT

Each living body, be it human, animal, insect, tree, or flower, star, planet, or galaxy, has a unique frequency that is measurable. This frequency reflects the degree of consciousness of the living body that it surrounds. The more conscious or pure of heart and mind we are, the higher we vibrate. The less "awake," conscious, and clear we are, the lower our frequency. The Earth and humanity are currently going through what is termed an *ascension* process. The Earth as a whole is ascending, which means her frequency is rising in response to an unprecedented increase in the influx of galactic energy. These intensified galactic frequencies also affect humans on physical, emotional, mental, energetic, psychic, and spiritual levels, as our personal frequencies respond to these incoming waves of energy and attempt to synchronize with them.

Many people are feeling these energies particularly strongly, both those who are "sleeping," and particularly those who are conscious, pure of heart and mind, and spiritually awake. The latter include souls who have volunteered at a higher level to transmute lower energies for the collective. The many who are "awake" and conscious are aware that before incarnating they chose to clear not only the remnants of their own karma but also that of the collective and the planet. The work of raising the collective vibration of humanity and of the planet as a whole is essential if we are to assure ascension.

The galactic energies that are permeating the energy field of the Earth and that of her inhabitants are impacting us globally, with erratic weather patterns and an increase in volcanic activity and tectonic shifts. Such activity is mirrored by the instability of governmental systems, which are beginning to collapse. Everything we understand about ourselves and our planet is changing. The increasing galactic frequencies will continue for a number of years to come, affecting us at a personal level, influencing the way we think and feel and the actions we take.

These higher frequencies are catalyzing our transition from a third-dimensional consciousness into a higher level of fifth-dimensional consciousness. Part of this "ascension" involves passing through the fourth dimension, the bridge between the third and the fifth. The fourth dimension is the level that supports the energetic changes within our aura or luminous energy field from a lower to a higher vibration. Known as the *transmutation* level, the fourth dimension is where we experience the accompanying transition symptoms, referred to as *ascension symptoms*. As the high frequencies permeate the physical body, they catalyze a necessary clearing and healing process to raise its vibration to a higher frequency. At a physical level what is occurring in the transmutation process is the creation of a new biological and biochemical blueprint, which will allow our cellular structure to hold a higher vibration.

People all over the world have been experiencing challenging, bizarre, and extreme physical reactions, which are mostly ascension symptoms. These symptoms include: exhaustion, shaking, dizziness, palpitations, breathing difficulties, intense nausea, migraines, headaches, body aches, hypo/hyperglycemic or diabetic symptoms, humming and buzzing in the body, IBS, chronic fatigue, long- and short-term memory loss, brain fog, slurring of speech, bladder/bowel weakness, sweating, ice cold shivers, burning heat, lethargy, hormone imbalances, and the sensation of being physically old beyond our years. Many are having extreme physical experiences, including accidents, having to be hospitalized, or taking time off work due to unexpected physical challenges. Others are enduring a continual round of physical symptoms, afraid to share the extent of their health challenges for fear of being labeled hypochondriacs. Evidence for this is to be found when we look at the fact that hundreds of thousands of people are linking through the World Wide Web, researching, sharing, and educating themselves about why it is that they continue to face challenging health problems with no verifiable medical diagnosis.

MY ASCENSION PROCESS
AND ACTUAL DEATH AND REBIRTH

My own ascension process began when I was sixteen. My impeccable health began to deteriorate around the same time that my psychic abilities rapidly increased. Twenty-three years later, on March 16, 2002, I collapsed with a mystery illness that threatened my life. That morning, as I got out of bed and stood up, my legs gave way. I became bedridden, as I could not walk unaided or withstand any sensory stimulation, such as television, music, or light. I remained in a room in complete silence unable to do anything and feeling as if I were dying. I was barely able to speak more than a few words. I could not sit up, as my body would not hold me upright and for a twenty-four hour period, I was unable to open my eyes at all. Nothing mattered to me anymore, not the books, clothes, or objects in the room. Everything was slipping away and I felt I must be dying. I lost interest in "normal" life as I lay alone, suspended between life and death.

Two weeks later, on Easter Sunday of 2002, I experienced the process of dying. The conscious experience of the physical body dying is unlike any other. To be conscious as the body dies, feeling each nuance of that process at a physical level, is beyond comprehension. I was losing consciousness and became aware of rapidly aging, experiencing myself as very old with long grey hair, skeletal, lying crumpled and lifeless on the bed at the point of death. This is the moment when I died to the life I had incarnated into. I aged decades in seconds, to reach the point of death I was destined to have experienced in this life. I experienced my own death fifty years ahead of time and in that moment, reincarnated, skipping the birth, toddler, child, teenager, young adult, and young woman stages, to arrive in my late thirties as my future self. This was made possible for me because of the relentless self-awareness and self-realization work I had undergone, which allowed me to skip this life and begin to live the next one.

This experience has proved to me that it is possible to reach into the future and draw the being of who we are destined to become into our current life, and live this as our new reality. Such an experience changes the whole life plan. Suffice to say, my life has never been the same since. Even though I am the same, I am not. It is so fascinating—when I look back on my life as a child, adolescent, and young woman it is as if I am viewing a past life. In fact I am, because I have lived two lives in one. From that point at Easter 2002, I began to anchor my future self more fully, a process that took several years.

Four years later, in October 2006, as part of this process of more fully anchoring my future self, I was inextricably struck down with extreme dizziness that persisted for twenty-four hours a day, seven days a week, for nearly two years. It rendered me unable to lie down at all because of the spinning and accompanying nausea. For the first year when the symptoms were with me throughout the day and night, this was terrifying and totally debilitating. In the second year the symptoms were ever-present though less extreme. By the end of the second year I was mainly affected severely with the dizziness when attempting to lie down. I had heard through several sources that it was around October 2006 that the Earth's etheric poles had reversed and I believe it is this energetic phenomena that caused such a reversal of energy within me. As the etheric stabilizes, so too does my own dizziness, and I imagine that in time, when the etheric process is fully stable, my own dizziness will disappear as my body becomes fully adjusted to and aligned with the influence of the reversed etheric poles.

As a result of my body becoming a little stronger, my future self was able to begin to anchor more fully into my body. The vibration of this is far higher than that of my previous energy and my body has been acclimatizing and adjusting to this higher frequency ever since. Time will indicate when my soul energy and physical body have synchronized, at which point I shall embrace the full purpose of my soul's calling.

ASCENSION NUTRITION

I discovered that ascension requires specific nutrients during each phase. Changes occur in the chains of our amino acids, some of which require proteins not found in vegetables. Foods that are high in cholesterol, including eggs and cheese, support the body's transformation. Our cells need a coating of cholesterol-based lipids or fats to hold a higher frequency and to hold the cell wall or membrane together. Many vegans and vegetarians find themselves in a dilemma, craving fish or animal proteins. Having been a vegan myself for twenty-five years, I found this to be my experience. Four years after I collapsed I suddenly craved fish, which at first I tried to ignore. However, my mind was flooded with images of fish, which would even wake me in the early hours of the morning. My body specifically craved mackerel and tuna, which I had never eaten. I agonized over the decision whether to begin eating fish until the intensity of my body's reaction made the decision for me. I surrendered to its wisdom. Now I allow myself to eat fish occasionally when my body requires it.

ASCENSION SYMPTOMS

This list has been gathered through my own channeled and physical experiences, in addition to other sources. Check and see which of these you recognize or are currently experiencing:

- An increase in psychic, mediumistic, clairvoyant, and intuitive skills.
- Acute sensitivity to negative energy around specific people or environments.
- Sudden extreme sensitivity to people or crowds. You may find that your once sociable nature suddenly disappears and you simply cannot bear to be with certain friends, family members, colleagues, or coworkers.
- A noticeable inability to tolerate someone with whom you have had a previously close relationship.
- Sudden inexplicable panic or anxiety attacks occurring at any time with no valid reason.
- Acute sensitivity to shopping centers or crowded environments such as restaurants, clubs, festivals, and so on.
- Extreme sensitivity to mobile and digital phones, laptops, computers, wireless routers, and all microwave technology, as well as certain types of lighting.
- Zoning out for long periods of time with an overpowering need to sit and do nothing. (This often occurs as a result of our consciousness spending increasing amounts of time in the fourth and fifth dimensions.)

- The need to rest and sleep for much longer than usual or sudden insomnia in normally sound sleepers.
- Falling asleep and then waking in the middle of the night at or around the same time, feeling wide awake and needing to be up, and oddly not being tired the next day as expected. (This is a sign of your consciousness adapting to new cycles of activity.)
- Strange electrical energy coursing through the body or body parts like legs or arms. (This is caused by the raised frequencies from the galactic center flooding the planet. These energies assist in the process of rewiring the physical and light-body in order to carry higher vibrating energies.)
- A whole range of physical experiences caused by detoxification as the body continues to release years of physical, karmic, emotional, and mental toxic waste, producing symptoms including: fatigue and exhaustion; pallor; swollen tongue; excess thirst; stomach upsets, including cramps, flatulence, and bloatedness; headaches, especially at the base of the skull and migraines with pains over the crown and in one or both eyes; muscle, neck, and shoulder pains.
- Dizziness, balance problems, and feeling spacey (triggered by being in higher states of consciousness).
- Shaking.
- Increased appetite, either putting on weight, maintaining it or losing it no matter how much or little you eat. (This is because the body needs huge amounts of fuel for the process of shifting from the third to fifth dimension.)
- Sudden cravings for foods and beverages you have not wanted or eaten for years or since childhood. (This helps us to release memories of stored trauma or connects us to a pleasant memory, which creates a momentary shift in our consciousness to enable a release to take place.)

Our Five Bodies

In addition to the physical body, we are composed of three subtle bodies, which can be described as part of the luminous energy field, and a causal body that can be likened to a "bridge" between the "earthly" subtle bodies and the more "spiritualized" levels that lie beyond. The subtle bodies become progressively more refined as we reach the spiritual realms.

1. The *physical body* appears visible to the naked eye and feels solid to the touch. It is the densest of all the bodies.

2. The *etheric body* is the first of the subtle bodies and closely mirrors the physical. It sustains the life of the physical body and is the location of the *chakras* (the energy centers located within the body). A complex and highly sophisticated structure of meridians runs from the etheric throughout the physical body, connecting to all major organs, glands, and nerves.

3. The *astral* or *emotional body* is the domain of the emotions and all emotional energy.

4. The *mental body* is the domain of the concrete mind, our thoughts, mental energy, and our left brain.

5. At its earthly level the *causal body* is responsible for the abstract mind, visionary art, creativity, inspiration, psychic vision, and the superconscious. At its spiritual level it represents the "higher triad," three levels beyond the subtle bodies that pertain to the soul or spirit (known as the atmic, buddhic, and monadic). These are referred to as part of the light-body.

The causal body is believed to remain with us throughout our many incarnations, whereas the physical and subtle bodies are newly created each time we incarnate. The causal body is the storehouse for all our accumulated obligations and rewards. It can transform our reality and it is to this body, not the mental body, that we must communicate the dreams and visions that we wish to manifest in our lives.

THE TWELVE PHASES OF
ASCENSION AND TRANSMUTATION

The ascension process takes place in a sequence of twelve phases. It is more than likely that you will resonate with the descriptions of the phases. You may experience many of the symptoms from different phases simultaneously or in a different order in your own ascension process. These twelve phases are based on personal experience and insights and information I have received from my higher Self and my spiritual guides. They also include many of the ascension phases described by Jasmuheen (of the Cosmic Internet Academy).

Phase One: You may experience extreme and debilitating exhaustion. Strong physical reactions to intense galactic energies can result in physical illness and symptoms. Your experience of these symptoms will depend upon the degree of emotional, psychological, and karmic clearing you have undergone. The more understanding you have of this physical clearing, the more you will be able to accelerate the process. Mild symptoms can be indicative of nearing the completion of a phase or may suggest that you are just entering the process. Intense symptoms suggest one of two possible scenarios:

1. A rapid and unprecedented clearing of ancient and historical stories held at a cellular and soul level. This can be an extremely challenging experience.
2. You are resisting the awakening process. If you are not implementing the required changes in your life then you may find yourself stuck, unable to move through or past the physical symptoms.

Phase Two: You may still feel mild flu symptoms and extreme tiredness. At times you can feel disoriented. At this point karmic experiences will be released and a space created within for the existential "Why am I here?" question. You may experience dizziness or problems with balance as light in the etheric releases structures that cause your emotional, mental, and spiritual bodies to spin. At this stage you experience rapid changes in all areas of your life.

Phase Three: Your physical strength returns. Your senses are refined and you experience increased sensitivity. Your body is resonating with a higher frequency.

Phase Four: As a result of the tremendous chemical and electromagnetic changes taking place within your brain, you may find you suffer from headaches, blurred vision, weakened eyesight, and hearing difficulties. Vision and hearing are being realigned for a different function. You may also have mild chest pains or infections, cardiac arrhythmia, increased pulse rate, higher blood pressure, and increased heart rate, as the heart chakra opens and expands. Always check any symptoms by having the appropriate medical tests, which will usually turn out to be normal. In this phase you experience inexplicable compulsions to follow Spirit without hesitation as the emphasis becomes: *Thy Will* not *my will*. You may also find you possess heightened intuition with flashes of telepathy and clairvoyance. This is the phase when you begin to master the emotional body.

Phase Five: At this stage the mental body attunes with Spirit. You experience lucid dreams, déjà vu, nonlinear thinking, and deprogramming and reprogramming of your old thought patterns. You shift from "reaction" to "response."

Phase Six: You begin to attract those with a similar vibration as your own. Many old contacts and friendships are outgrown and left behind as you manifest "soul family"—peers and co-creators. You re-evaluate your life, your job, relationships, environment, home, and lifestyle. You are aware of the desire to let go of the old, to write new stories for your life that are not the scripts handed to you from others. You feel elevated, lighter, and free. At this stage your body is capable of holding thirty-five percent light. Living by your intuition feels natural.

Phase Seven: The heart chakra begins to expand. You joyfully sense your authentic Self. You continue to experience a release of deeper levels of emotional residues. You begin to lose your emotional attachment to others. At this level you overcome fear as you align with the heart. Pressure at the forehead and at the back of the head occurs as the pituitary and pineal glands expand and open. At this phase you can simultaneously experience joy and fear as you seek more of the former and less of the latter. Your relationship with Spirit deepens and you may wish to leave the planet to merge fully with Divine Love. Remember you are needed here! By realizing that you can be on the Earth *and* be in joy, you experience a desire to create a completely different life. You eat less and prefer lighter foods. You drink more water in preference to other beverages.

Phase Eight: You wish purely to be of service. You leave the "saving and rescuing" mode behind in favor of the desire to serve Divine Will. The pineal and pituitary glands change shape. (If headaches persist ask the Beings who are working with you to simply "tone it down," for they do not feel pain, or ask them to help you to "release endorphins," the brain's natural opiate.) The brain is being activated, particularly the cerebrum, the "sleeping giant." Cranial expansion is common; triangular "seed crystals" in the brow and recorder crystals in the right side of the brain are activated along with the eighth, ninth, and tenth chakras. You begin to be hooked into the languages of light. The pituitary and pineal glands are opened fully and work together to create the "Arc of the Covenant," a rainbow light that arcs over the top of the head to the third eye, which is a decoding mechanism for higher-dimensional language. You may find it hard to find words to express yourself as you may think in geometries, tones, or abstract ways. If confused, ask for messages to be decoded and translated. Again you become much more aware of the vastness and multidimensionality of your nature, aware that you can be anything that you want to be. You cease to operate from obligation and relationships become transpersonal. You share words from your heart and soul; others may feel disoriented when dealing with you as they no longer have "hooks" into you. You have heightened sensitivity and awareness, yet feel grounded and serene.

Phases Nine to Twelve: These phases are the process of transmutation from Homo sapiens to Homo luminous. They are described in detail in chapter six.

ACTIVATING THE LIGHT-BODY

We have reached a critical juncture, at both a human and planetary level, as we journey through these remaining years to 2012. For millennia ancient prophecies have foretold a time when future humans would transform into bodies of pure light. The Maya, Incas, Hopis, Egyptians, Tibetans, Sufis, and Alchemists all speak of the ultimate transformation of the human form into light.

The first eight stages of the ascension process shift the third-dimensional human body into a fifth-dimensional body, where our consciousness, vibration, and frequency are aligned with fifth-dimensional higher energies (the ultimate goal of the ascension process). The transmutation process that follows transforms the human being from *Homo sapiens* to *Homo luminous.*

The Incas and Native Americans make reference to the coming of a "new human," having a "rainbow body" that is fully healed and in which each of the main seven chakras fully radiates its particular intense color. A part of our soul journey is to fulfill these prophecies by beginning to activate the light-body, which connects us directly to the higher realms and fully with our souls. The consciousness of most people operates from the aura, where core trauma origin imprints and the genetic blueprint are located. However, the light-body contains our divine blueprint; when we access it we become transformed and catalyze the next level toward *enlightenment* (liberation from the lower self and reconnecting with Source).

The aura/luminous energy field that surrounds our physical body is shaped like a doughnut with light pouring through the center. Energy flows through the body then rises from the feet up the body to the crown, where, like a fountain, it spills out, running down the outside of the body as an incredible swirling mass of energy and activity. In a healthy individual this doughnut-shaped energy field is at its most expansive when we are in nature. However, when we are in a city or a big town, the doughnut shape constricts and acts like a tight sheath around the physical body.

For better or for worse, whatever is contained within our luminous energy field dictates our life experience. It contains the imprints of our early life experiences, genetically inherited predispositions to illness, womb memories, and memories of former lives. Trauma that is not healed the instant it occurs becomes encoded with a charge and embeds into the aura. This "charge" consists of the energy of the trauma, as well as its information. A particular energetic "story" can be triggered at any time, as can a myriad of other embedded stories. When this occurs, the trauma energy and information leak into the central nervous system and take it over. This catalyzes a psycho-energetic reaction, which triggers themes similar to the original trauma wound. As the trauma seeks to heal, we find that we will attract the same patterns over and over again until such a time that we recognize and respond to the deeper purpose behind the experiences. *We recreate our history in order to heal now what could not be healed back then.* It is important to understand that the repetitive nature of patterning serves to retraumatize us, magnifying the imprints and entrenching them even further into our aura. The aura becomes toxic when these "trauma imprints" leak toxins and collect in "pools," which begin to debilitate us and anesthetize our consciousness.

Trauma = Imprint = Compromised Luminous Energy Field = Illness

If we seek a physical cure through pharmaceuticals or surgery without clearing the aura, then it is most likely that our symptoms will re-occur. However, we do not need to continue to recreate past traumas in our current lives. If you experience any kind of trauma and upheaval, stress or anguish, anger or sadness, then these are symptomatic of "trauma." The times we now live in present us with new ways to heal and evolve. We need to listen to what the aura is trying to teach us through the symptoms that we are presented with. If we are willing to learn these lessons we enter into a conscious partnership with the imprints and our lives are no longer at the mercy of unresolved and unhealed trauma. We can then *respond* to what we discover, choose to cultivate inner peace, let go of the details and free ourselves to experience life in a unique and magical way.

THE MUNAY-KI RITES

Shamanic practices, the most ancient healing modalities dating back some fifty-thousand years, offer us powerful ways to clear the luminous energy field, ultimately resulting in the activation of the light-body. This ancient healing wisdom, which has been passed down through the ages, includes a vast amount of alchemical and magical practices. One in particular, the Munay-Ki Rites, has the express purpose of catalyzing the clearing and healing of the aura. The term *Munay-Ki* comes from a Quechua word, which translates as "I love you."

First brought to the Americas by the Laika, who crossed the Bering Straits from Siberia some 30,000 years ago, the Munay-Ki rites derive from the great initiations of the Indus Valley. According to the Q'ero (Incas) these rites were first given to ancient teachers and elders by angelic beings. The Laika, known as the Earthkeepers (stewards of all life on the Earth) of old, knew that people would come to the Munay-Ki rites when they were ready. Those most drawn to the rites are the people who long to change their lives and to make a difference to the world. The ninth rite, the "Creator Rite," was transmitted to humanity for the first time in the summer of 2006 at the Holy Mountains in the Andes. Before this it had not been available to human beings.

The nine Munay-Ki rites of initiation are energetic codes that can be downloaded into the light-body. These nine stages assist us to heal at a deeper level and reconnect with the core essence of who we. As the rites clear the luminous energy field of emotional trauma imprints, they raise our vibration. As this happens we are directly connected to the presence, wisdom, and guidance of the Luminous Ones. They draw closer, recognizing that we have a common vision and mutual calling. The presence of these beings gives us access to knowledge that helps to catalyze the transmutation process from *Homo sapiens* to *Homo luminous*. Their guidance can help us to see future possibilities and the potential for humanity. Earthkeeper wisdom tells us that "We can be influenced by who we are becoming."

Receiving the Munay-Ki rites clears the chakras to enable each energy center to be fully infused with its original color, rather than remaining the dull grayish pool of psychic sludge that many chakras have become. This is a result of layers of accumulated trauma, not only from this life but also from many previous lifetimes. Once each spinning wheel of energy returns to its original color (from base to crown: red, orange, yellow, green, turquoise, indigo, and purple/violet), we have acquired what the Earthkeepers describe as a "rainbow body."

Below are listed the nine Munay-Ki rites of initiation as explained by Alberto Villodo, medical anthropologist, shaman, and founder of the Four Winds Society (www.thefourwinds.com).

The First Rite consists of protections installed in your luminous energy field. These are known as the Bands of Power and consist of five energetic bands representing earth, air, fire, water, and pure light. These bands act as filters, breaking down any negative energies you may experience into one of the five elements. These energies can then be a resource for you instead of making you toxic or ill. The Bands of Power are always "on," and any negative energies will be deflected. In a world filled with fear, the bands provide essential protection.

The Second Rite is the Healers rite, which connects you to a lineage of Earthkeepers from the past who come to assist you in your personal healing. We have tremendous spiritual assistance available to us. These luminous beings work on us during our meditation and sleep time to heal the wounds of the past and of our ancestors.

The Third Rite is the Harmony rite, in which you receive seven archetypes into your chakras. In the first chakra you receive the archetype of serpent; jaguar goes into the second; hummingbird into the third; and eagle into the fourth. Then, three archangels go into your upper three chakras. Huascar Inka, the keeper of the lower world and the unconscious, is transmitted into the fifth chakra; Quetzalcoatl, the feathered serpent god of the Americas and keeper of the middle world (our waking world) goes into the sixth; and Pachakuti, the protector of the upper world (our superconscious) and keeper of the time to come, goes into the seventh chakra. These archetypes are transmitted into your chakras as seeds. The seeds germinate with fire, and you have to perform a number of fire meditations to awaken them and help them grow.

Afterward, they help to combust the psychic sludge in your chakras so that they can shine with their original light as you begin to acquire a rainbow body. This rite helps you to shed your past in the way a serpent sheds its skin.

The Fourth Rite is the Seer rite. This rite installs filaments of light, which extend from the visual cortex in the back of your head to your third eye and heart chakra. This practice awakens your ability to perceive the invisible worlds.

The Fifth Rite is the Daykeeper rite. The Daykeepers were the masters of the ancient stone altars found in sacred places throughout the world, from Stonehenge to Machu Picchu. The Daykeeper is able to call on the power of these ancient altars to heal and bring balance to the world. This rite is an energetic transmission that connects you to a lineage of ancient Laikas. According to lore, the Daykeepers called on the Sun to rise each morning and set each evening, made sure that humans were in harmony with mother Earth, and honored the ways of the feminine. The Daykeepers were the "midwives" who attended births and deaths, as well as being the herbalists. They were generally women and were knowledgeable about the ways of the feminine Earth. This initiation begins the process of healing your inner feminine and helps you to step beyond fear and practice peace.

The Sixth Rite is the Wisdomkeeper rite. The legends say that ancient wisdom resides in the high mountains. The ice-covered peaks of South America were revered as places of power, just as other mountains around the world, from Mt. Sinai to Mt. Fuji and Mt. Olympus, have been honored as places where humans meet the Divine. Wisdomkeepers are medicine men and women from the past who defeated death and stepped outside of time. The job of the Wisdomkeeper is to protect the medicine teachings and, when appropriate, share them with others. This rite helps you to step outside of time and experience infinity.

The Seventh Rite is the Earthkeeper rite. This rite connects you to a lineage of archangels who are guardians of our galaxy. They are reputed to have human form and said to be as tall as trees. The Earthkeepers come under the direct protection of these archangels and can summon their power when needed to bring healing and balance to any situation. The rite of the Earthkeepers helps you to learn the ways of the seer and to dream the world into being.

The Eighth Rite is the Starkeeper rite. This rite anchors you safely to the time after the great change that is predicted to occur on or around the year 2012. According to lore, when you receive this rite, your physical body begins to evolve into that of Homo luminous. The aging process is slowed down and you become resistant to the diseases you were once vulnerable to.

The Ninth Rite is the Creator rite. When you receive this initiation you awaken the God-Light within. You acquire stewardship for all of creation, from the smallest grain of sand to the largest cluster of galaxies in the universe. This rite became available on the planet for the first time in 2006. Although there were individuals who attained this level of initiation and awakened their Christ or Buddha consciousness, it was never possible to transmit it from one person to another until now. So, while Spirit-to-human transmission happened on occasion, human-to-human transmission was impossible.

During the actual transmission of the Munay-Ki rites, the lineage of Luminous Beings is conveyed from the head of the teacher to the head of the recipient as their foreheads meet during the initiation. The Munay-Ki rites can only be given by those who have directly received them from another initiate. Once you have received these rites you are then able to transmit them to others. However, there must be no charge involved. If the rites are a part of a healing practice and you charge for the other healing modalities you work with, then it is acceptable to include the Munay-Ki rites. However, the actual transmissions must not be charged for. Receiving these rites accelerates our development. Because of this, issues may come to the surface to be processed. Working with a skilled and qualified therapist who is familiar with this particular healing method will help you to process what may arise for you. (See resource directory for contacts.)

When we have received the seventh, eighth, and ninth initiations we are able to download and anchor an upgraded blueprint—a divine blueprint—in exchange for our old genetic one. This new blueprint *enlightens* the light-body, which in turn activates our DNA with new, upgraded information, which transforms our experience of physical life in terms of how we heal, age, and even how we choose to die. The nine rites of initiation constitute the totality of attunements required for us to experience transcendence from our current human form to a body of light.

INNER PEACE AS A PRIORITY

We can make gentler and more respectful choices. Make an agreement with yourself and others not to get caught up in details. Let the details go. Make an agreement with yourself to cultivate a state of inner peace as a priority, one that you are not willing to compromise. By developing a new approach to what is required for our healing we can begin to experience how it feels to remain centered and peaceful. This is not only a liberating experience, but an excellent one for our ongoing physical, emotional, and mental health.

We can learn to approach our emotional wounding and the healing we need in a new way, one that calls for us to respond rather than to react. In psychotherapy, our emotions are often symbolized by water.

Using this as an analogy, imagine the experience of treading water in a calm ocean in contrast to being tossed about on a stormy sea. An incident with His Holiness the Dalai Lama offers a wonderful example of a person maintaining his equilibrium. At an important gala dinner he was seated at a table enjoying a conversation, throwing his head back in laughter, as he is often known to do. One of his Tibetan assistants approached him and proceeded to whisper something into his ear. Onlookers observed the Dalai Lama's face transfigure in seconds from an expression of boyish delight to one registering intense pain as he heard the news he had received. Within a matter of seconds he had processed the news and returned to his jovial self, becoming once more fully present to his guests.

This process is the action of a highly developed soul who embodies inner peace and an absolute unattachment to "details." The Dalai Lama has the ability to fully process an unpleasant experience in moments, allowing it to wash through him and register at every level, then to finally emerge with equilibrium restored. This exemplifies mastery over the emotions and the mind. We too can remain centered when encountering stories of tragedy and suffering, be they our own or those of other people. Let us choose a different way to respond to our own life stories and the impact they have upon us. Above all, we can choose to prioritize a state of inner peace. We can choose to walk in peace, to talk peace, to think, feel, and act in peace. To radiate peace. To be peace.

CHAPTER FIVE

Earth's Entrainment
with the Galaxy

It is my personal belief that the time is quickly approaching for the maturation of the god-seed and global lightbody activation leading to a hypercommunication revolution with the ability to unite all of humanity as an enlightened consciousness. "The age that has been written about, whispered about, and spoken about is upon you," writes [Barbara] Marciniak. "It is the age when humanity physically mutates and literally turns into something it was not a short time before multidimensional beings." For the ancient Incas, our generation, which is fortunate enough to experience the "end of history" with the Galactic Alignment of 2012, is poised to become the true chakarunas, *"the bridge people" tasked with creating Heaven on Earth.*

SOL LUCKMAN, *CONSCIOUS HEALING*

As we have already seen, the ancient Mayan civilization was one of the most astronomically advanced in human history. Their Long Count calendar is the most accurate to date on the planet. According to it we are currently "between worlds," as the Mayan fifth world finished in 1987 and the sixth world begins in 2012. This period of "between worlds" is foretold as the time of "Revealing" or "Apocalypse," meaning that truth will be revealed. The Mayan sixth world is blank, without prophecy; it is up to us to co-create a new world of our choosing.

This time of change has been referred to as the "Time of Great Purification," "Shift of Ages," "Great Shift," "Great Transition," and so on by many peoples of the Earth including the Maya, Hopi, Sioux, Egyptians, Kabbalists, Essenes, Q'ero, and Aborigines. One of the defining characteristics of this time is the entrainment of the Earth with the galaxy. According to Wikipedia, entrainment is "the process whereby two interacting oscillating systems, which have different periods when they function independently, assume the same period." This is a process in which the Earth is aligning more and more with the galaxy, in terms of vibration and frequency, unlike at any other time in known history.

The solstices from 1999 until 2012 (twenty-six in all) denote a time of great change and intensity as humans receive and integrate new galactic energies. During a solstice, large quantities of solar and galactic energy pour into the Earth's magnetic field through either the North or South pole of the Earth, depending on which is tilted toward the Sun; at the summer solstice (in the northern hemisphere) the North Pole is fully tilted toward the Sun and the situation is reversed at the winter solstice.

Each solstice invokes a reprogramming of the magnetic planetary grids of the Earth, as well as the activation of specific light codes, invisible frequencies that download higher-dimensional messages and information into the psyche of the individual through the causal body. The causal body informs our DNA and divine blueprint, thus activating the superconscious mind and higher triad of the atmic, buddhic, and monadic levels and catalyzing the transmutation process of the human being toward becoming Homo luminous.

The influence of each "downloading" lasts for six months until the next solstice, when we receive more advanced light codes and consciousness programs from extradimensional intelligences and solar and galactic influences. This is giving humans an unprecedented opportunity to raise their consciousness and transmute their physical bodies at a cellular level. We entered the "home run" with the summer solstice on August 11, 1999, at 11:11 a.m. GMT, which was in alignment with the galactic plane, close to the galactic center. This resulted in an attunement of the Earth to the energies emanating from that center.

The thirteen-year period beginning in 1999 is also described as "the Quickening" and you may have noticed that time appears to have speeded up as we race toward the winter solstice of 2012. A number of other Earth changes are occurring, which correlate with prophecies that foretell of the evolution of the Earth and of human consciousness. They include hypercommunication, crop circles, and magnetic pole reversal.

HYPERCOMMUNICATION

I am using the term *hypercommunication* to describe forms of communication that are beyond our present norm in third-dimensional reality. They may include channeled information from ascended masters, extraterrestrials, or angelic beings, channelings or connections to collective consciousness or the Akashic Records, interspecies communications, such as with dolphins and whales; they may also include communications from discarnate spirits with their own agendas. Another form of hypercommunication occurs at the galactic level via "wormholes," shortcuts in spacetime, connections that link entirely different areas of the universe through which information is transmitted outside of the time/space reality. Hypercommunication is dependent on DNA to receive the data that streams into the group consciousness of the Earth from sources outside third-dimensional consciousness.

Hypercommunication is a natural process and is responsible for sudden flashes of information and insights that are ordinarily outside of our accessible knowledge. The state of hypercommunication is most pronounced when we are in a state of deep relaxation, in a heightened state of consciousness, or in a hypnogogic/trance state. Anxiety, stress, and mental overload can block our ability to pick up sparks of these transmissions or we can interpret what we pick up in a distorted way or with no significant meaning.

Various forms of hypercommunication phenomena have been utilized by nature for millions of years of evolution. Here is an excellent example of how hypercommunication can be seen at work. When a queen ant is spatially separated from her colony, building work in the nest continues fervently and according to plan. If the queen is killed, however, all work in the colony stops. Not a single ant knows what to do. Apparently, the queen transmits the "building plans" through a process that is not dependent upon her being in or near the colony. Far away from the colony, via the group consciousness of her subjects, she is still able to send the information needed. The queen can be any distance away as long as she is alive.

Several sources suggest that in earlier times human consciousness acted as a group consciousness. In the belief systems of many ancient cultures (such as the Maya, Greeks, and Hindus) it is said that our consciousness was highly evolved in a previous Golden Age. At that time our collective consciousness expressed as *unity* consciousness. The tunnels that link us directly to the universe were once a natural part of our awareness. Hypercommunication information, light language, and light codes passed through them unobstructed. This previous Golden Age was an era of great peace, advanced consciousness, evolution, and group connectedness to multidimensional realities.

However, as we descended into duality consciousness and separateness, our DNA atrophied. For thousands of years we have experienced a third-dimensional consciousness, which vibrates at a low level, and the tunnels of light information exchange have been mainly dormant for a long time. We have almost completely lost our capacity for hypercommunication. To explore and experience duality, the descent in consciousness was a necessary and vital part of the evolution of the human soul. Now, as we find ourselves on the threshold of another Golden Age, we can regain a state of unity consciousness and access to information from many dimensions via our DNA. As an analogy, the Internet (representing our

DNA) is an apt example of a data network and superhighway that unites and mirrors the imparting of information via group consciousness.

My Own Experiences with Hypercommunication

In June of 1997, at around six in the morning when I was in an hypnogogic state (just waking), I heard a whooshing sound that circled my head a few times and then entered my left ear. I felt what I can only describe as an intense voltage course through my body, as if I were being plugged into the generator of a city. My body felt as if it would explode into a billion pieces.

During this experience I was unable to physically move. Even though I was conscious and awake I could not open my eyes; my face was contorting and my sacral chakra felt an unbearable pressure, as if it would burst. I could hear a loud "humming" sound and my mind felt like a tornado, with powerful buzzing sensations rushing through it. Exactly one month later the same experiences were repeated and then again the following month, after which they began to occur weekly and then daily.

One of the things that would happen during the experiences is that I would "see," "hear," and "travel" while the energy was in my body. I found myself flying over vast stretches of land, mountains, and oceans; I traveled far out into the dark heavens of our galaxy at great speed and through portals to other dimensions. I gained profound information and insights that have been of enormous benefit ever since. For example, in 2000, I was told of a "constellation" called "Ophiuchus." At the time I had no idea why. I had never heard of it before. Nine years later, having given this experience no further thought, I had a rush of hypercommunication relating to Ophiuchus while writing this book (the importance of which I explain in more detail later in the chapter).

The hypercommunication was always cryptic and intensely surreal. On one occasion, I was "visited" by an other-worldly being with turquoise eyes who told me of something yet to come in my life. I wait to see if this unfolds during the next two years. I became accustomed to astral traveling (in the nonphysical realms of consciousness) and experienced being conscious and awake while in a light trance, my astral body (the nonphysical counterpart of the physical human body) levitating in the room and "traveling" out into hyperspace. Nothing that I was shown or experienced was ever threatening or frightening. I would know in advance when this energy was arriving, as I would hear an intensely hypnotic "whooshing" sound. After a couple of years that sound was replaced by a more powerful buzzing sound and sensation. I felt I had a choice and I could stop this from happening by sitting up and forcing my eyes to open. However, this was not easy, as the buzzing sound was overwhelmingly hypnotic.

The energy that coursed through me was indescribable. It was like a powerful voltage with currents pulsing through my body like electrical tsunamis. The closest I have come to seeing anything similar to this was in a scene from the movie *Phenomenon* when the main character is struck by a heavenly beam of light, knocked to the floor, and left twisting and vibrating in an uncontrollable manner. Unsure of what was happening to me, I endeavored to contact numerous mediums, psychic institutions, and channels. I even consulted doctors and specialists, but to no avail; no one understood what I was talking about. I wondered if I was having night/morning fits and, at my request, a doctor referred me to a neurologist. The specialist sat perplexed and suggested I was suffering from narcolepsy, a sleeping sickness where people fall asleep on the spot day or night! Of course, this was far from the case, as I could control what was happening, remaining conscious throughout and none the worse for the experience. In fact, I would feel quite energized and well following these almost daily episodes.

The final two experiences of the energy surging through my body occurred in April 2002 and November 2002. During both of these, for the first time since I was six, I experienced a "psychic attack," when an outside energy imposes its will upon a living human being. Shortly before these final two episodes I had collapsed and almost died. At the time of these two specific attacks I was very ill, resulting in my vibration being very low and rendering me vulnerable to psychic attack and not being able to move through the astral realm. What I experienced was terrifying. Two androgynous entities, deathly white with bright red mouths, sat on top of me with their hands on my throat trying to strangle me, while laughing hideously.

During the second attack in November 2002, I realized that I needed to recite sacred mantras to try and raise my vibration so they would let go. After that final attack, I promised myself that I would never allow that energy access to me again. If Spirit wanted to work through me they needed to respect my boundaries and value my choice to continue this journey in a different way, which is what has occurred; I have not had one of these experiences since. I have heard the buzzing, hypnotic sound a few times since but it immediately disappears when I state firmly "No" and in that I feel very respected.

Do not be concerned that your own process will be harrowing or include such experiences. I had invited these experiences to myself. In early 1997, I began earnestly praying to Spirit to be used as a channel. Little did I know at the time that in order for me to do this I would be required to go through a death and rebirth experience so that my whole system would shut down to allow me to rebirth a new body from the old. Undoubtedly, those five years of incoming energy, followed by seven years of unrelenting and harrowing illness, proved a transmutation at every level of my being, which served my soul's evolution and purpose. When the energy was in my body, I experienced the unimaginable with extraordinary insights, visions, and indescribable sensations. Hypercommunication works differently for me now, flowing through my energy body receptors and translated by my mind, instead of coming directly into my physical body.

CROP CIRCLES

Crop circles are another expression of the Earth's entrainment with the galaxy. It is estimated that ten thousand crop circle formations have appeared all over the world in recent years, appearing with increasing frequency mainly in England, but also America, Canada, Australia, Japan, Russia, China, Germany, the Netherlands, Austria, Brazil, Romania, Hungary, and many other locations. Approximately two hundred and fifty crop circles appear around the world every year. Even though these crop designs occur on a global scale, they are predominantly found in the Northern Hemisphere with Salisbury Plain, Wiltshire, in England, being the main location of activity.

Crop circles have provoked much scientific enquiry and yet continue to defy scientific explanation. Neither botanists nor scientists are able to explain how these formations appear without causing any damage to crops. They acknowledge that authentic crop circles cannot be duplicated by human attempts. Crop circles have taken on a mystical meaning and seem to suggest a communication from an intelligence or consciousness beyond third-dimensional reality. They display scientific, astronomical, and esoteric symbolism in intricate and precise geometric shapes and designs. Some shapes appear to denote dates and astronomical conjunctions, while others remain obscure and are open to interpretation. Some appear to reflect multicultural symbolism. Many crop circle formations relate to fractal geometry. The Mandelbrot Set, which appeared in 1991, is considered one of the most famous; it was deemed to be a perfect representation of one of the most complex shapes in mathematics.

The appearance of crop circles seems to be seasonal, as most formations appear in the three main summer months. Crop circles appear mostly in barley, corn, and wheat, as well as canola oil (rape seed) fields, although they have been found in rye, oats, flax, pea, and potato crops, as well as rice paddy fields in Japan and in wild grass and undergrowth. During a forty-five minute period on a summer's afternoon in the UK in July 1996, a 915-foot spiral of 151 circles appeared opposite the ancient sacred site of Stonehenge in Wiltshire, England. An aircraft pilot, security guard, and gamekeeper confirmed that no such formation had been apparent at five thirty in the afternoon and yet just after six in the evening the enormous formation appeared. How could this be possible in just thirty minutes? On August 13, 2001, a crop circle formation appeared on Milk Hill, Wiltshire, England. Said to be the largest formation to ever appear, it consisted of 409 individual circles in a spiral pattern. The size and complexity of this formation is staggering. It puts the hoaxer theory into perspective, for, if made by humans, then a circle would have to have been created every thirty seconds throughout the night for this design to appear by sunrise!

The crop circle phenomenon has created intense debate; the most common interpretation is that the formations are communications from extraterrestrials. This suggestion is made more credible by the many sightings and video footage of UFO activity close to each location at the time of new formations. Scientific tests have shown biological changes taking place at a cellular level, suggesting the involvement of microwave energy. Authentic crop circle formations alter the electromagnetic field of the locations in which they are formed, rendering cellular phones, cameras, and batteries inoperable and compasses unable to locate North. Aircraft equipment fails while flying over the formations. Crop circles have been witnessed as they have appeared, with people describing remarkably similar experiences. There are approximately thirty or so different observers who all talk of "a high pitched whistling sound," "lights," and an "invisible powerful and tangible energy" that arrives out of nowhere, spinning the crops with great force and yet creating little or no damage. Witnesses tell us that the whole sequence of events is completed in a matter of seconds.

Channeled information suggests that crop circles are a "frequency" and that the symbolism is a "language" that is being implanted on the Earth's surface. The geometric symbols are establishing a certain frequency that is set to increase. These symbols represent an evolved intelligence that has the capacity to communicate vast streams of highly complex codes and information. Sound frequencies, which are beyond the human capability to detect, are catalysts for the evolution of our consciousness. Channeled sources also tell us that the circles are interconnected designs, forming an intelligent grid-work around the planet, which will hold a frequency that humans can utilize in order to evolve. This higher intelligence language is not yet fully present on the Earth, as the "downloads" respond to the level of consciousness and overall frequency of humanity.

The crop circle phenomenon is another form of hypercommunication. Speculation is that long ago human DNA was changed by damage to the higher circuits of the human genetic system, which resulted in a more primitive way of existence. What the crop circle patterns may be doing is recreating and reconnecting our genetic circuitry, acting as a "firing mechanism" to stimulate and recreate DNA programs of genetic instruction. This may create specific waveforms and template-like webs of intelligently focused energy to alter consciousness in a certain way. As hypercommunication develops and evolves, we will be able to contact super-intelligent galactic and universal life forms and receive direct conscious communication and transmissions into the individual and collective energetic fields, bodies, and minds. Crop circle formations serve as tangible physical evidence of this.

Crop circles, sacred sites, and ley lines (scientifically proven straight fault lines in the Earth's tectonic plates) have a much lower magnetic field than other areas and therefore support phenomena such as hypercommunication and other altered states of consciousness that open us to information outside of our usual knowledge and experiences beyond our normal perception. For those who wish to explore hypercommunication, visiting such places will support changing states of consciousness, which may trigger hypercommunication experiences.

SCHUMANN RESONANCE
AND MAGNETIC POLE REVERSAL

The *Schumann Resonance* is named after German physicist Professor Winfried Otto Schumann, who calculated in 1952 that electromagnetic "standing waves" are formed in the space between the ionosphere and the Earth's surface. This was confirmed in 1954, with the detection of resonances with an average overall global frequency of 7.83 Hz. This electromagnetic "pulse" is generated mainly by the combined effect of worldwide lightning discharges, which release a very high frequency (VHF) between 1 kHz to 30 kHz, followed by a very low frequency (VLF), below 2 kHz. Their combined effect produces electromagnetic waves, which circumnavigate the Earth. In addition to the average very low frequency constant of around 7.83 Hz, there are frequency harmonics of 14, 20, 26, 33, 39, and 45 Hz; these are known as the "Schumann Resonances."*

According to Wikipedia, Nikola Tesla was the first to research the existence of this fundamental frequency in 1899. For thousands of years the Schumann Resonance, known also as "the pulse of the Earth" or the "Earth's heartbeat," has been steady at 7.83 cycles per second. It is not strictly true to call Schumann resonance the "Earth's heartbeat." It is more like the "pulse" on the surface. Of course this is a manifestation of the heartbeat, which originates within the Earth's electromagnetic iron core. The Schumann Resonance is so consistent as an accurate measure of time that the military uses it as a reliable point of reference.

However, according to Gregg Braden, geologist, author, and researcher, since 1980 this pulse has slowly accelerated to the point where it is now over *twelve* cycles per second, twice what it was in the mid-1980s.† Instead of the twenty-four-hour day we have been used to, we are now experiencing what amounts to a sixteen-hour day. Every cell in the physical body is trying to synchronize with this accelerated pulse to keep time with mother Earth. This explains why we experience days, weeks, months, and seasons as seeming to "fly by."

At the same time, according to Braden, the Earth's rotation is slowing. His research shows that the Earth's electromagnetic field has dropped forty percent in the last 2,000 years, six percent occurring in

---

*See www.earthbreathing.co.uk/sr.htm.

†In personal communication October 21, 2010, Gregg Braden noted "We know more about Schumann now than we did twenty years ago. The Schumann Resonance has changed and consists of multiple harmonics of frequencies; the second harmonic is now dominant. There are layers of frequencies that make up the composite Schumann cavity Resonance; these layers are dynamic and not static." For further information please refer to the GCI website with HeartMath, www.glcoherence.org.

the past 100 years. He suggests that when the Earth slows its rotation to a point of near standstill and the resonance frequency reaches thirteen cycles, we will be at a *zero point* magnetic field. At this point the Earth will stop rotating and, following a period of two to three days, will begin turning again in the opposite direction. This will produce a reversal in the magnetic fields around the Earth, after which they will begin to grow stronger.

The end point of the Mayan calendar may well be connected to this imminent magnetic pole shift. Most sources agree that the last full reversal was about 780,000 years ago, although the average time between reversals is only 250,000 years. Thirteen thousand years ago there was a magnetic field shift known as the Gothenburg Flip, which was not a full pole reversal, so we are overdue for another full reversal at any time. Scientists have calculated that the poles are not due to reverse for at least another two thousand years; however, they measure time in a linear fashion. Time is not linear; it is cyclical, which means this date is inaccurate.

We see the results of this declining magnetic field as global warming and erratic weather patterns across the world. If we add the acceleration of the Earth's pulse to the declining magnetic field, we begin to realize that the Earth is undergoing tremendous changes. So too are our bodies, for we are made of the same matter. Whatever the Earth experiences within her body, we also experience in ours. Metaphysicians and quantum physicists acknowledge this and the term "ascension symptoms" is how our increasing physical challenges are described. Our bodies must adapt to Earth's lowered magnetic field. This will make it more possible for humans to naturally access altered states of consciousness. Scientists tell us that the frequency of the Earth is identical to the alpha-wave rhythm of the human brain. Others believe this frequency is also the resonant frequency of the human body. As this frequency alters, so too does our consciousness and evolution.

During the 1960s, Robert Monroe, a pioneer of out-of-body experience (OBE) research, began to have spontaneous out-of-body experiences, when the consciousness leaves the confines of the physical body. Monroe claimed to have heard different frequencies that he believed triggered the OBEs and so began research on the effects that these could have on various states of consciousness. Monroe felt he could help to induce OBEs in others. After much experimentation, he deduced that the brain resonated to different frequencies when exposed to the various pulsations of sound waves. Monroe and his team of researchers at the Monroe Institute in the United States have shown that out-of-body experiences occur when the body's electromagnetic field lowers dramatically and then reverses.

Geoff Stray (author of *Beyond 2012: Catastrophe or Awakening? A Complete Guide to End-of-Time Predictions, The Mayan and Other Ancient Calendars,* and *2012 in Your Pocket*) poses an important question concerning the pending zero point of the Earth's ionosphere. He asks, "If the Earth's magnetic field reverses, would this trigger out-of-body experiences for the mass of humanity?" This is an interesting point to consider. Guidance tells me that when the Earth's magnetic field drops to zero point, human evolution will move to a higher level of consciousness.

NUMERICAL CODES AND THE EVOLUTION OF HUMAN CONSCIOUSNESS

In metaphysics and esoterica the numerals 11:11 are considered to represent a *numerical code* pertaining to a cosmic portal. According to Solara, author and facilitator of the 11:11 Planetary Activation in 1992, in which over 144,000 people participated worldwide, the 11:11 portal opened on January 11, 1992. Many metaphysicians and researchers believe that since then this portal has been downloading higher-dimensional energies, frequencies, and light codes onto the Earth, which have been activating our pre-encoded cellular memory. Solara suggests that the 11:11 portal is due to close on November 11, 2011, at which point we will reach the completion of the 11:11 cycle. Between then and

January 13, 2013, our pre-encoded cellular memory will be preparing to download a new and important numerical code: 13.

It is interesting and informative to notice how often certain numbers, such as 11 and 13, occur regularly in significant ways. For example, the Mayan Long Count calendar, also referred to as the 13 baktun cycle, lasts for approximately 5,125 years (the numbers of which add up to 13). John Major Jenkins, eminent Mayan researcher, points out that the 13 baktun cycle is the fifth and final one of the 2,600-year precession of the equinoxes.

The Significance of 11

In numerology, 11 is considered a master number. The configuration of 11:11 is of immense significance in numeric coding. Many people have noticed their attention being drawn to the 11:11 numbers on digital clocks, watches, mobile phones, and other display units showing digital time. Our DNA is encoded and at specific times is triggered by numeric codes as well as the changing frequencies that switch us on, raise our consciousness, and awaken our higher minds. The number 11 represents the spiraling twin strands of human DNA that are currently being activated in order for the next stage of human evolution to begin. 11:11 is one of the "wake up" codes that activate our DNA and trigger the superconscious mind and our soul memory, as well as our genetic coding so that we will remember our true nature as multidimensional spiritual beings.

The total solar eclipse of 1999 occurred at exactly 11:11 a.m. UT (Universal Time). The winter solstice of 2012 (completing a thirteen-year cycle) occurs at exactly 11:11 a.m. UT. Terrestrial time, based on the atomic clock, the most accurate measurement of time, which takes in variations of the Earth's rotation, places the exact moment of the eclipse at 11:13 a.m. GMT. So which one of these times is correct? Even though terrestrial time will register 11:13 a.m. on the atomic clock, it is exactly the same time as 11:11 a.m. UT. It is fascinating that not only do the two times of the 2012 winter solstice revolve around the numerals 11 and 13, but also the momentous 2012 winter solstice occurs at exactly the same time as the solar eclipse of 1999. There are no coincidences.

The Alchemy of 13

Contrary to the "unlucky" association that the number 13 carries, this alchemical numeric code represents unity, union, interconnectedness, and Oneness. While the number 12 represents the circle and the completion of consciousness, symbolic of our individual move toward unity, 13 represents the spiral and transcendence, a quality that is beyond the realm of physicality. The Maya associated it with the *mysteries* and divine manifestation. The number 13 always holds the point of greatest power and the digits below take their place around it. This can be illustrated by Jesus and his twelve disciples. The disciples acted as twelve separate points of consciousness revolving around a single point of focus, Jesus, to blend with and become one consciousness. Similarly, King Arthur was the thirteenth among his twelve knights.

For over 5,500 years the Maya, Incas, Druids, Egyptians, and Essenes followed a thirteen moon calendar, which is still used by those who align with a galactic system of time. In 1933, the League of Nations actually voted for a thirteen-month calendar to be the new world standard because of its reliability and continuity. The thirteenth month was to be called "Tricember," but this was blocked by the Vatican, the very organization that imposed the Gregorian calendar on us over four hundred years ago.

While the year of 2012 is a profoundly important moment in itself, it also acts as a bridge to 2013, the year that marks the beginning of what the Hopis call "the Emergence" (humanity's shift from duality to unity consciousness). As we research and explore 2012 phenomena, we discover that the digit 13 is ever present.

OPHIUCHUS: THE THIRTEENTH SIGN

From the beginning of time people have looked to the stars for guidance. The Babylonians invented a solar-lunar calendar that alternated between twelve and thirteen months, as the constellations were unequal in size. Eventually they divided the zodiac into twelve equal divisions, which have remained unchanged despite the movement of the constellations that occurs over time. Historical references suggest that the Babylonians were aware of thirteen constellations but chose to exclude Ophiuchus as part of their zodiacal system. A thousand years later, around the time of Plato, the ancient Greeks discovered astrology and astronomy. Plato campaigned for Ophiuchus to be included in the Greek zodiacal system but to no avail. Two thousand years later, we still use the Greek zodiac of twelve signs to plot the movement of the planets, stars, and constellations in the heavens.

The thirteenth sign, Ophiuchus, is located in the center of the Milky Way. Because of its position, it is said to govern the other twelve signs of the zodiac. This sign is known as the "Serpent Healer" or "Serpent Holder" and is represented by a male figure holding a serpent. On November 13, 2012, there will be a solar eclipse involving the Earth, the Sun, and the head of the serpent. Could it be pure coincidence that the constellation of Ophiuchus becomes activated just thirty-eight days before the end of the Mayan calendar? What exactly does Ophiuchus contribute as we begin the home run of the end of one age and into the beginning of another? Could the November 13 eclipse prove to be the shedding of a skin for humanity? Is this a transmutation of human consciousness, as represented by the serpent? The total solar eclipse near Ophiuchus may well facilitate the crossing of the momentous 2012 threshold from dark to light, a pivotal transition in human history when we shed the old and are reborn into the new world.

This particular eclipse will open a portal for the incarnation of a group of highly evolved serpent-linked souls, who can be referred to as "Ophiuchuns." Also known as the Thirteenth Rainbow Tribe, they were prophesied by the Maya and the Native Americans. Serpents played a central role in traditional Mayan culture and cosmology, representing knowledge, wisdom, and energy. The Mayan temple of "Palenque of the Inscriptions" is also known as the "Temple of the

Gestation," because in the upper part of its five entrances stand columns carved with figures in the shape of Mayan priestesses carrying babies. The infants are shown to have one human foot, while the other appears to be a serpent. The women are depicted holding the babies with one hand and the head of the serpent with the other. These same inscriptions were carved in the pyramid of Lord Pacal (Votan) and the Maya wrote more than 2,500 glyphs of reference, which are found near the stucco figures.

The serpent children were prophesied to be the "children of the future," who would bring great wisdom, knowledge, and energy to the Earth. These "serpent" beings follow three generations of consciousness transformers who have been incarnating since the 1930s (see chapter ten). The first generation are known as the Lightworkers; the second, who began to incarnate in the early 1970s, are referred to as the Indigos; they were followed by the Crystal souls who arrived in the 1990s. The Rainbow souls are predicted to start incarnating en masse from 2012 onward. They were prophesied to reincarnate into an era when the cosmos and the constellation of Ophiuchus would support their arrival, at a time when the world is most in need of their unique gifts. That time is upon us.

The ancient Maya knew that humanity would enter a long and sustained period of ignorance and darkness. This is the time that we are now living in. Mayan experts have established, through interpreting ancient Mayan inscriptions, carvings, and hieroglyphics, that ancient Mayan initiates learned about these serpent-race prophecies and it is probable that many of those initiates who lived thousands of years ago will reincarnate among the waves of Rainbow beings arriving from 2012 onward. On December 30, 1999, Pluto, the planet representing transmutation, regeneration, death, rebirth, and renewal, met Chiron, the healer (ruler of Ophiuchus), in the thirteenth constellation and downloaded specific codes into the Earth's grids in preparation for activation at the winter solstice of 2012, when the first major wave of Rainbow souls will incarnate and fulfill the Mayan prophecies.

The Luminous Ones have expressed that whatever transpires post 2012, these beings will still incarnate. If by that time we have not managed to transcend the dark path we are currently on, then the role of the Rainbow tribe will alter to address the escalating crisis of the planet and humanity. If, however, we are able to transcend to unity consciousness, these Rainbow beings will be instrumental in building upon the foundations laid by the previous three generations of consciousness transformers. They will continue to establish the new world that will have unfolded following the winter solstice of 2012.

The solar eclipse of November 13, 2012, will also initiate our planet into the mysteries of Ophiuchus, activating a portal through which new information, light codes, and frequencies will be transmitted. This new information, pouring into the grids, will permeate our energetic bodies and consciousness at multidimensional levels, as well as penetrating the energetic structure of all living matter. We can think of this as similar to what takes place in the neural pathways of the brain at certain key points in our development. There is a natural closing of old neural pathways, to allow other neural pathways to open in response to the new information they are receiving.

These new galactic codes will anchor into the planetary grid to further the collective evolutionary journey for humanity and the Earth. As the Earth's grids are upgraded with new codes and information, this also affects the overall evolution of the galaxy, the cosmos, and the universe. Ophiuchus, the heavenly shaman/healer, acts as the catalyst for the activation of vital codes to accelerate our consciousness and vibration, as well as our personal and collective healing. These codes will be specific to the frequency of 13, the numerical digit that represents the mysteries. They will bring advanced information, as yet unknown to humankind, which will be released from the planetary grid in 2013, a year that is now being hailed as *the year of the unknown.*

It appears from my research that, apart from the prophecy of a golden age of peace, there are no specific or detailed prophecies of what will unfold after 2012. The year 2013 presents humanity with a "blank slate" on which we can write a new script. In 2013, we will find ourselves in a unique and extraordinary position, one which liberates us from the past and allows us the opportunity to create a new vision for the future.

Ancient prophecies speak of a "star gate" opening in 2012. They tell us that there are thirteen of these gates in our galaxy. Star gates are often described as "wormholes" or "portals" and it is prophesied that a great enlightened being or a group of enlightened beings will emerge from one that will open on the winter solstice of 2012. The Maya refer to these openings as "serpent ropes" on which enlightened beings are said to "ride in." These ropes are linked to the kundalini energy within the human body; when they are fully activated, via the heart/mind connection, they open up portals and wormholes within the human system, making it possible for ourselves, as the enlightened beings that we are, to "ride in," fully anchoring our souls into our bodies and re-aligning our consciousness to elevate our vibration to an exalted state. The profound events of 2012 make it possible for us to turn our faces to the Sun and bathe in the golden dawn of a new age.

CHAPTER SIX

Four Generations of Consciousness Transformers

Lightworkers, Indigos, Crystals, and Rainbows

There will be a tear in the fabric of time itself, a window into the future through which a new human species will emerge. They call this new species, Homo luminous.

ALBERTO VILLOLDO, *TIMEWAVE 2013*

Transformers of consciousness have been incarnating throughout human history. In the past, they have been noticeable as single beacons of light, including Mohammed, Krishna, Buddha, and Christ, or small focused groups dotted around the world at any given time. However, since the mid-1930s a mass wave of souls began to incarnate. They represent the final four phases of the twelve phases of ascension presented in chapter four: Lightworkers, Indigos, Crystals, and Rainbows. Let us now begin our exploration of understanding these "way-showers," who blaze the trail and show humanity how it is possible to evolve from thousands of years of history as *Homo sapiens* into a new type of human, *Homo luminous.*

LIGHTWORKERS

Masters—Pioneers—Revolutionists

Lightworkers are highly advanced souls and are pioneers for the transformation of human and planetary consciousness. Lightworkers began incarnating around 1935 with a mass wave arriving in the early 1940s. This influx continued until the early 1970s. Their mission and reason for incarnating was to act as catalysts for the turning point of humanity, which would ultimately lead to the transformation of human consciousness in 2012 and beyond.

Many of these advanced souls incarnated with a great degree of karma to resolve and heal at a personal level. They have chosen to clear all of their karma in this incarnation so that they will no longer need to incarnate on Earth. If they manage to fulfill their personal and worldly quest, they will have a choice about whether or not to return to this planet to play a supporting role at a global level in future lives. Many Lightworkers have attained high positions in the public domain and appear to lead somewhat dysfunctional personal lives as they struggle to heal their personal karma. But by honoring their voluntary role of carrying the torch for the evolutionary journey of humanity, they will have liberated themselves from the wheel of death and rebirth, as their contribution to human and planetary consciousness will have proven to have been invaluable. If they do choose to incarnate again, they will be free of karma and the struggles they may have endured during this lifetime.

Many of these evolved souls incarnated during wartime, with a specific mission for peace. They revolutionized society and the world, most notably in the 1960s, through a creative and spiritual uprising. These advanced souls acted as a bridge between the materialistic West and the spiritual East. Lightworkers who came into adulthood in the 1960s triggered a cultural revolution and led us into the peace-loving early 1970s. They encouraged us to "Turn on, tune in and drop out"—to turn on to another way of being, to tune into ourselves, and to drop out of the rigid, repressed class-based system that had ruled for hundreds of years. Today, we still revere some of these war babies as great cultural icons. It is important to acknowledge their often undervalued contribution to the world in which we live today.

We only have to recall the 1960s to feel the undeniable and incredible energy that marked that decade as unique, one whose influence still echoes loud and clear to this present day. To have lived through and been a part of the 1960s revolution must have ultimately been a blessing. The 1960s stands out as pivotal in the West's cultural evolution. However, we are now about to enter a decade of unprecedented change, a unique window of time that, like the 1960s, will change the world forever. That time is NOW and leading up to and beyond 2012.

INDIGOS

Of the many seeds sown by the Lightworkers throughout the seventies, some blossomed in the wombs of these pioneers of human consciousness. The children of Lightworkers who incarnated from the 1970s onward came to be known as Indigo children. The children born before this time to early Lightworkers are what are termed *second wave* Lightworkers, born with similar missions as their parents or other Lightworkers who might have been significant influences as they were growing up. Most Lightworkers did not incarnate through Lightworker parents because of the karma they needed to heal. They incarnated into circumstances that, regardless of how difficult, provided the perfect emotional and physical environment for their soul's healing and growth. Mass waves of second wave Lightworkers incarnated between 1960 and 1970.

Indigos are defined by an intense Indigo blue energy field or aura and are born into the Indigo ray of consciousness and evolution. They are highly intuitive and psychic, as well as artistically gifted, techno-logically brilliant, with a more integrated balance between left and right hemispheres of the brain. Nancy Ann Tappe, an early authority on Indigo children, called them "Children of the New Millennium," "The Blue Children," and "Children of Light."* She coined these terms because of the characteristic blue color of Indigos' electromagnetic field, a phenomenon that can be captured with Kirlian photography. Nancy Ann is described as having a rare brain disorder called synesthesia, a condition that mixes up the five senses to create odd experiences such as "hearing shapes" or "tasting sounds." Nancy is therefore able to see col-ors vividly. Nancy Ann explains that Indigo children tend to be more intelligent than "normal" children, that they learn faster, they are not afraid of or discouraged by adults, they know what they want and will fight to get it.

The majority of Indigos incarnated during the period of the early 1970s through to the mid-1980s. These souls have brought with them advanced abilities in the fields of technology and creativity. A whole generation of Indigo adults are now in their twenties to mid-thirties. These advanced beings are preparing and being prepared to take their place as leaders of a new world beginning December 21, 2012. The Indigos have a vital role to fulfill in shaping the world to come, espe-cially in the areas of feeling and intuition. They are important new paradigm teachers in the fields of metaphysics, quantum physics, eso-teric knowledge, advanced sciences, and technology. The Indigos are here to teach us not to rely so much upon the spoken or written word, but to develop new ways of communication, which will be faster and more direct (think Internet broadband as opposed to dial-up). They are here to teach us how to communicate more honestly and to develop our capacity for telepathy as we begin to explore the medium of "mind to mind" communication.

---

*Nancy Ann Tappe, *Understanding Your Life through Color: Metaphysical Concepts in Color and Aura.* Starling Publishers, 1986.

CRYSTALS

Crystal children began to incarnate on Earth from about the year 1990. They convey an extremely powerful presence and intelligence. Their main purpose is to guide humanity to the next level in our collective evolution to reveal our divine inner power and intelligence. Crystal souls differ from Indigos in that they function more as a group consciousness rather than as individuals, and they live by the "Law of One" or unity consciousness. Crystal beings exemplify the union of the will, love, and peace, and radiate this through their intensely magnetic presence. They champion empowerment for all and feel a sense of mission to lead people into unity consciousness.

Crystal children have a predominant feature of penetrating hypnotic eyes that can see deeply into the person their gaze is set upon. Their eyes display a wisdom far beyond their years. They are telepathic and will teach this natural gift. Crystal children have a happy disposition and seem to delight in everything or everyone they encounter, having an unconditional capacity to forgive. These children tend to develop the ability to speak late, often not talking until three or four, or sometimes even years later. Crystal adults will really begin to flourish after 2012.

Like Indigos, Crystal souls are sensitive, psychic, intuitive, and highly intelligent emotionally. The main difference between Indigos and Crystals is in their temperaments. Indigos have a fierce warrior spirit, with an enormous capacity to cope and excel in challenging situations. They understand when truth and integrity are lacking and hone in on that with absolute precision. It is this gift that makes it possible for them to bring about resolution to any situation. Indigos are assigned the role of deconstructing any system that no longer serves humanity. They will challenge duality-based systems including government, media, education, legal, and financial institutions. In contrast, Crystal children tend to be easy-going and quite enraptured by nature and the stars. One could define the Indigos as the trailblazers and reformers who expose and rip out the old institutions and the Crystals who follow in their path with the purpose of establishing new foundations built upon peaceful action. Both are here for a specific purpose, which is to assist humanity and the planet in the great transition from third- to fifth-dimensional consciousness.

Crystals have brilliant gold luminous energy bodies, which also contain magenta rays. They are masters of light and sound, creative geniuses who excel in communication. Crystal children will express a desire to learn about the higher aspects of physics, such as quantum physics, or metaphysics. Ideally they need an educational environment that can respond to the needs of these special souls and support them through childhood. These children are often mistakenly judged as being lazy, uncooperative, or unintelligent due to their failure to be interested in third-dimensional subject matter in the current schooling system. Many of these beings are now adults, or approaching adulthood, introducing new philosophies and reintroducing ancient wisdom. Crystals naturally align with the new world leadership style needed post 2012.

THE THIRTEENTH RAINBOW TRIBE: POST 2013

A new generation of consciousness transformers will begin to incarnate en masse from 2013: they will be the thirteenth Rainbow Tribe, prophesied thousands of years ago by the Maya and the Native Americans. The Cree have a prophecy that very clearly states this.

> There will come a time when the keepers of the legend, stories, culture rituals, myths, and Ancient Tribal Customs would be needed to restore us to health, making the Earth green again. The Rainbow Warriors will show the peoples that Great Spirit is full of love and understanding and teach how to make the Earth beautiful again.

Native American ancestors also spoke of:

A time when the Earth would become very sick and that because of the unrelenting greed of the new culture the Earth would fill with deadly liquids and metals, the air would be rendered foul with smoke and ash and even the rains, intended to cleanse the Earth, would plummet in poison drops. Birds would fall from the sky, fish would turn belly up in the waters, and whole forests would begin to die.

They go on to say:

Under the symbol of the rainbow all of the races and all of the religions of the world would band together to spread great wisdom of living in harmony with each other and with all the creations of the Earth. Those who taught this way would come to be known as "the Rainbow Warriors." Although they would be warriors, they would carry with them the spirits of the ancestors, they would carry the light of knowledge in their heads and love in their hearts and they would do no harm to any other living thing. After a great struggle, using only the force of peace, these rainbow warriors would finally bring an end to the destruction and desecration of Mother Earth and peace and plenty would then reign through a long, joyous, and peaceful golden age.

In the words of Lee Standing Bear Moore of the Manataka American Indian Council:

Among the few who possess inner strength to resist the mass unconsciousness will rise a new neo-indigenous people. Prophecies foretell of a people who will rise from Earth's ashes like the thunderbird, symbolizing rebirth. They will bring balance and harmony back to Mother Earth. The first of these beings will come as teachers and storytellers to remind us of the ancient truths of the star people and beyond. They will be pathfinders leading the way to a new universe, a new reality. Warriors and Shamans of many nations will be born and they will cleanse the Earth for rebirth. Next will come the Planters sowing seeds of truth, justice, and freedom. The Storytellers, Warriors, and Planters will live in the way of the Great Spirit and teach ways to keep Mother of the Ground sacred forevermore. They will be called Rainbow Warriors for they will gather the four sacred directions, all distinctly separate but forever connected in the Circle of Life.

Many Native American prophecies align with other indigenous ancient wisdom teachings to pinpoint 2012 as the year of the fall and of the rise, of an end and a beginning, of a death and a rebirth. The Earth is in desperate need of the thirteenth Rainbow Tribe.

Crystal souls are said to be the future parents of the thirteenth Rainbow Tribe who will begin to incarnate en masse from approximately 2013 to 2030. The luminous energy fields of the thirteenth tribe are imbued with all the colors of the rainbow. Some Rainbow beings, known as "scouts," are already here to open and prepare the way for those to come. Throughout all the generations of consciousness transformers there have been such "scouts" who have arrived a few years or decades before the arrival of mass waves. The Rainbow scouts are noted as being great child healers or gifted children whose abilities are beyond explanation or understanding in our present time, for they are aligned with the necessary changes required in the collective consciousness.

Rainbow souls have no personal karma and are here to teach, heal, and guide the collective and the Earth in the coming golden age. The children of the thirteenth Rainbow Tribe will bring great joy and harmony to the families they incarnate into and will spread that love and joy throughout the world. This generation of highly evolved souls will have an undeniable wisdom. In their younger years they will display a marked development of love, understanding, and forgiveness. These evolved beings will have a tangible and noticeable aura of light. When they become involved in any situation they will literally light up all around them, uplifting the atmosphere purely by their presence. They are the teachers of teachers of compassion, love, forgiveness, and wisdom.

Many of these beings to come have never previously incarnated. Their purpose is not to heal at a personal level, but to facilitate global and collective healing. They will hold great wisdom. They will specifically choose parents who vibrate at a high frequency, hence it is unlikely that they will be found in "dysfunctional" or lesser evolved soul groups or families. These beings will be totally trusting, yet not naive. The trust they will feel for everyone and everything will come from their ability to see straight into the heart of another, a situation, or issues in the world. Rainbow souls will complete what their Crystal parents, Indigo grandparents, and Lightworker great grandparents set in motion.

The Lightworkers and Indigos role is to help to midwife the old paradigm into the new, which leads us up to and over the 2012 threshold. The Crystals are here to help to build upon the new foundations of the newly emerging world. The Rainbows will then carry forward the new paradigm, building upon the foundations laid by the Crystals. The thirteenth Rainbow Tribe will be role models for unconditional love. Whether you have children or not, look around you for the Indigo, Crystal, and soon-to-arrive Rainbow children.

The spiritual teachings for humanity have always been the domain of adults. However, these children will be the new teachers of the *next level* of consciousness and will teach new ways of expressing unconditional love. This unconditional attitude of loving-kindness aligns with the expression of "Christ consciousness," which will come to the forefront as we shift from duality to unity consciousness. Rainbow souls will also be known as "Christed children" who fully express fifth-dimensional Christ consciousness. From early times we have been taught to respect our elders. We need to also respect the young, for many are reincarnated ancient elders as well as very advanced souls from higher dimensions. We need to ensure that we give a voice to the galactic wisdom held by this younger generation who are here to help lead the way into the future.

As the parents, guardians, and caregivers to this new wave of souls, it is vital that we support them so they may unfold to fulfill their destiny. It is important that we respect who they are and support what they will be here to achieve. Rainbow children will be known by a marked difference in their nature and their self-expression. They will be wise beyond their years, aware from an early age of the role they are here to fulfill. Such children will tell *you* who they are. Rainbow souls will fully embody their purpose from around 2030 to approximately 2050.*

THE NEXT LEVEL FOR LIGHTWORKERS

Prophecies handed down from the ancient Americas foretell of a "new human" appearing on the planet: "One who lives free of fear, one of great wisdom who lives in their eternal nature." Lightworkers have been on a long and arduous road to raise global awareness, consciousness, and personal and planetary vibration since 1935. This role continues to remain the priority for all four generations of consciousness transformers. However, the evolutionary role of Lightworkers is now to spearhead the shift from Homo sapiens to Homo luminous, the transformation of humans into beings of light, while remaining in physical form.

The groundwork put in place by Lightworkers is all but done and their souls no longer have this as a priority. Many Lightworkers are experiencing extreme fatigue and feel worn out, battle weary, as they near the end of the group task to prepare the ground and lay the foundation stones for the emergence of a new paradigm, a new world. Many Lightworkers are now noticing that a change is occurring. The restrictions and blocks that have been ever present, which have prevented the manifestation of personal hopes and dreams, appear to be lifting. Vast numbers of Lightworkers are reporting direct experiences of the powerful energy of change in their lives, as the lights that have for so long been on red or amber are now switching to green. They are now very close to the next stage of their soul contribution and evolution.

---

*The Diamond souls will also begin to incarnate in this time frame. The purpose of these souls is to align human consciousness with the Diamond mind, which will emerge during the mid to latter part of the twenty-first century. I will say more about the Diamond souls, who themselves pave the way for the ultraterrestrials and the interuniversals (highly evolved superintelligent beings and energy forms that exist and travel between universes), in my next book, *Beyond 2013: A New Blueprint for an Evolving Humanity*.

CHAPTER SEVEN

For the Highest Good of All

Our challenge, which is also a tremendous opportunity, is to open up to a literally life-changing way of thinking ourselves into existence.

SOL LUCKMAN, *CONSCIOUS HEALING*

You can let go of the old. Everything that unfolds in the next few years will support you in doing so. As the old world dies and gives way to the new, so too will our sad and painful memories, which belong in the old paradigm built upon fear. The new world is built upon love. You can choose love right now. *Fear or Love?* The choice is yours.

EMBRACING A NEW ROLE

You do not need to be Gandhi, Mother Teresa, or the Dalai Lama to leave your mark on this world. You need only an open heart and a willingness to let go of all that has gone before that may have caused sadness and pain. Step into a new role, a new you, a new life that will turn your whole world around and surround you with love, as you commit to a new way. Choose to let it all go now. Forgive and forget. Understand how those you perceive have hurt you were themselves hurt by others. Recognize that at a soul level, you chose the circumstances of your life in order to learn, heal, and evolve.

The origins of the wounds we carry are from lifetimes. We incarnate with these wounds and, at a soul level, choose to encounter those whose actions catalyze us to resolve and heal our soul wounding. From the soul's perspective, the perpetrators of our suffering are those with whom we have important soul contracts, the purpose of which are to remind us of what we need to learn about ourselves. Our perpetrators are our allies, not our enemies; they serve our soul's growth and healing.

Before we incarnated into this dimension many of us volunteered to "midwife" the birth of the higher vibrating fifth-dimensional Earth. The fact that you are reading this book suggests that you are one who has volunteered to assist the world in the special transition taking place now and leading to December 2012. This Clarion Call urges those of us who know we have a role to fulfill, yet feel this to be just out of reach, to step forward. This call specifically invites you to take a leap of faith and find the courage to move beyond the small self, fully embracing the incredible being you truly are.

This is a Clarion Call to those who recognize the importance of the times we live in and the responsibility that we each carry to overcome that which inhibits us so we can unite for a greater cause. This is a call to those who feel ready to embrace the gifts they have to offer to humanity and the planet, and who recognize that they have chosen to incarnate with a specific contribution during these incredible times.

Humanity has been afflicted with an all-pervading amnesia created over a period of thousands of years, as a result of living at a lower level of consciousness. What has long been forgotten is the true meaning our lives have, and what we have to offer to others and to the world. Our unique gifts and talents can contribute to the collective journey of our global family in these momentous times.

The higher realms are calling for us to *wake up* and *remember,* to remember what we volunteered to contribute. It is so easy to be distracted, sidetracked, and to put off to tomorrow what can be done today. We must recognize when we do this and ask ourselves, "How does it serve us to do so?" How does it serve you to focus your attention elsewhere? In what way does it benefit you to block your path to a life that feels alive with meaning and purpose? We were each born to shine. Your contribution to the world will bring you many gifts and a deeper level of fulfillment.

Time is of the essence and this is an eleventh hour Clarion Call to those who are prepared to respond. By committing to our roles, uniting with like minds to acknowledge the momentous Earth changes and transformation of human consciousness due to be catalyzed in 2012, we will truly know how it feels to experience Oneness as we shift from duality to unity consciousness with All That Is.

Preparation for and commitment to our new roles is now essential. We have less than two years remaining before the prophesied Shift of Ages. The important question is: "Will we reach the great destiny that awaits us?" The answer to this is up to us, both individually and collectively. Ancient elders tell us that human energy will be the deciding factor in whether we manifest a catastrophic outcome or one of unprecedented peace from 2012 onward. It is our human and spiritual responsibility to do everything we can now to assist in raising planetary vibration and consciousness.

CO-CREATING A NEW WORLD PARADIGM

No one really knows what will happen toward the end of December 2012. While much depends on our individual work and process, it is possible that an event could occur in which everything will transform in a single moment as we collectively awaken to Oneness consciousness. Alternatively, the transformation of consciousness could be a gradual process, the initial shifts subtle at first, obvious only to those who are sensitive to energy, vibration, and frequency.

Remember a time when you decided to change where you were living. You did not physically move the instant you had made the decision to do so. However, on all the nonphysical levels—emotionally, mentally, and energetically—you moved the moment you had the thought. The same may be said of the coming 2012 transition. When you consciously choose to recognize the significance of unfolding events and make a choice to support these, your awareness will have already shifted to the threshold of 2012, even though you physically remain in the present moment.

Returning to the house-moving analogy, physically you needed to prepare to move from one house to another by packing up the things in your old house before closing the door and crossing the threshold into the new. Crossing an evolutionary threshold also requires organizing and planning. What of your old ways do you wish to take with you and what do you choose to discard? Making such changes requires you to find assistance and support to ensure a smooth and easy transition.

Our new world requires us to live in a place of greater awareness and understanding. The new Earth calls for us to live a more exalted state of being, in an *elevated state of consciousness*. Those actively engaged in lighting the path toward 2012 will be responsible for providing the available resources for healing and the raising of human consciousness, services not exclusive to those who can afford them. As the prophecies remind us, our choices will determine the unfolding of 21 December 2012. We need to be willing to provide our support for exchanges other than money. For the world to transform and unfold into the prophesied Golden Millennium, access to ancient wisdom, rapid methods of healing, support, and guidance must be available to all. For a new paradigm to unfold that serves the highest good of all, without judgment, we need to let our hearts rule our heads. The way of the new world is *the way of the heart*. The heart is the compass by which we navigate our way toward and into a world built on peace, equality, truth, and love.

Only time will tell what will transpire. Following 2012, fundamental shifts will take place and, like the Tower card in the tarot, the old paradigm will fall and crumble, resulting in some disturbance and a necessary clearing process. We have inspirational prophecies that inform us that uniting with a higher purpose will ensure a positive outcome. We have enormous support from our *unseen* friends in the higher realms. The rare astronomical alignments and cycles set to culminate in 2012 will further support the emergence of a new world paradigm. It is up to us. If we make this shift into the Golden Age that the Hopis speak of, in a conscious manner, then the world will transform at a rapid rate.

It is possible that the post-2012 world may appear to be the same, with the existing global systems still in place. However, the changes will have occurred at a deep level, reaching into the core structure of the Earth and within the human psyche. The old ways that preceded the Shift of Ages will fall to the ground like autumn leaves, eventually turning to compost and inadvertently preparing the soil for new life and the emergence of the new world. Just as new seeds and bulbs are already sprouting below the surface of decaying foliage resting upon the mid-winter ground, heralding the promise of a new season, a new divine planetary blueprint will have been anchored into the deepest levels of the planetary grids and human psyche. As the months and years unfold post 2012 it will become evident that *everything* has changed.

Ancient wisdom cultures, as well as many other nations, gather regularly to pray for peace on Earth. These ancient and wise ones are adept at tracking possible future outcomes for the planet. They journey to the future to seek one where they find clean rivers and oceans, pure air, and people who live in harmony and unity with each other and with nature. The purpose for tracking and locating a desirable future as a possible outcome is to install it into the collective destiny as well as anchoring it as a future blueprint for the planet. This new blueprint is already in existence and has been for hundreds of years, even though the majority of humanity currently resides in the old blueprint.

When I ask my guides to share more with me regarding this, I am shown a pyramid where, at the pinnacle, ancient wisdom resides together with profound spiritual truth. Within this peak exists the consciousness of highly advanced beings. Their wisdom infiltrates the consciousness of highly evolved souls located just beneath them who have the task of infiltrating the consciousness of those awakened souls beneath them. They are able to translate complex spiritual language and codes, conveying them to the levels of consciousness that exist in the remaining lower portions of the pyramid. In this way the upper portions influence the lower ones. The higher we aspire, the closer we move toward the apex of the pyramid. Conversely, the less evolved and conscious we are, the nearer we exist to the base. Our current collective consciousness represents the widest and most dense band of the pyramid structure located in the lower to middle regions. The upper areas are where we find the consciousness transformers and at the tip of the pyramid are located the spiritual guides and teachers of humanity from this world and beyond. The fifth-dimensional blueprint held in the top section of the pyramid will filter down over time and eventually transmute the existing third-dimensional blueprint.

As we move into 2013, the unknown future, our ongoing commitment to an era of peace on Earth is essential to enable the divine blueprint of the new Earth to begin activation. Once it is established there will be no going back to third-dimensional living. The new Earth will be underpinned by unconditional love, elevated consciousness, compassion, empathy, honesty, kindness, equality, unity, inspired creativity, cooperation, collaboration, co-support, appreciation, gratitude, and nonviolent communication, in addition to other positively expressed heart- and soul-centered qualities.

It is *vital* that you understand what you are here to contribute and how to do this, even if it is impossible for you to grasp the bigger picture in terms of prophesy, quantum physics, astronomical events, or the existence of the limitless multidimensional beings who guide and help us each step of the way. What is required is the willingness to *open your heart* to all sentient beings and to *forgive those who have trespassed against you.*

Forgiveness:
Activating the Energy of Healing of Self and Other

A beautifully simple technique to help you to work on forgiveness is a modern version of an ancient Hawaiian Huna healing method known as Ho'oponopono. In this practice four short sentences are repeated with feeling: "I am sorry. Forgive me. I love you. Thank you." This can be done with specific individuals in mind. Or the phrases can be said without focusing on anyone in particular. This enables the healing of deep unconscious soul wounds that may go back lifetimes.

By elevating your consciousness, and being conscious in thoughts, words, and deeds, you will serve the higher good. It does not matter who you have hurt or how you have been hurt. This is a time of redemption. You have an extraordinary opportunity to be free of pain and suffering. Ultimately, the single most important requirement is your willingness to act with love toward yourself, everyone, and everything. The laws of the universe ensure that your soul will be rewarded in equal measure to your contribution and your ability to remain heart-centered, loving, and kind toward yourself and others. The energy of forgiveness, together with your willingness to raise your consciousness, will bring many unexpected and beautiful gifts into your life.

Acting As If

Acting as if is a powerfully effective practice to foster a new way of expressing yourself. In order to *act as if,* you first think of one person who inspires you, someone who is an exceptional example of unconditional love, acceptance, and nonjudgment. This will be a person who you experience as an inspiration, someone who conducts himself or herself in an exemplary and refined manner and who is kind and forgiving. You may or may not know this person. It may be a spiritual figure, family or community member, or someone whose life story inspires you. You might also find that by listening to my audio-therapy CD *Retrieving Destiny: Encountering Your Future Self* you will find all the inspiration you need for *acting as if* in your future self.

To act as if entails emulating the individual who inspires you. In certain situations you act as if you were that person. At first, *acting as if* may feel uncomfortable, yet it will be of enormous benefit to the world. If practiced over a period of time, *acting as if* will lead you to your true Self, for what you found so inspirational about your role model was really a reflection of yourself. By aligning your consciousness with the image, conduct, or experience of the person who most inspires you, by asking yourself when challenged by life, "What would this person do in the same situation?" "How would they respond?" "What would they say?" and then emulating this behavior, you will connect to the wisdom already held within you, as well as help humanity by your willingness to change.

Acting as if, in a positive and loving way, closes old negative neural pathways and opens positive new ones. *Acting as if* sends powerful signals and new messages to the unconscious mind. *Acting as if* re-informs every cell of your body, alters brain chemistry, and reprograms conditioned behavior. *Acting as if* is a preliminary to the profoundly transformative *lost mode of prayer,* of which I will speak later (see chapter twelve).

☽ Master in the Heart Reflection/Future Self
This beautifully simple exercise is a profound method of absorbing the vibration of a great master and integrating his or her influence into your way of being.

1. Close your eyes and turn your attention inward. Follow your breath as it leads you to your heart. Allow yourself to rest in the stillness of your heart.
2. Slowly begin to create a picture of a perfect being. This may be a spiritual figure, someone you aspire to emulate, or it could be your future Self. Begin to intensify the image or feeling of that being until you can see or feel him or her as vibrant and alive in your imagination or felt sense.

3. Place the energy and the image of this perfect being in your heart. Deepen your connection by inviting his or her energetic presence into every cell in your body.

4. Set an intention to be guided by the grace of the master's presence. Ask this being to walk with you as a role model in all endeavors and encounters. Choose to respond emotionally and mentally as you imagine this person would. Love in the way he or she would love. Allow your thoughts to reflect those of the master in your heart. Invite this perfected being to be the role model for how you respond to yourself, to others, and to life.

5. Invite the energy of this beautiful being to envelop your light-body and to permeate your physical body, bringing the gift of self-healing and an enhanced ability to heal others. By inviting the energy of this highly developed being into your heart, you heal your heart, attain a higher vibratory field, and can radiate loving-kindness out to the world.

6. When you are ready open your eyes.

If you practice this every day over a period of time you will absorb the vibration of the master in your heart and integrate his or her influence. By doing this you will begin to transform, and increasingly resemble the being of great wisdom who resides in your heart.

Carry this energy in your heart as if it were a precious jewel. Express gratitude for the gift of something so exquisite and perfect.

CHAPTER EIGHT

A Tomorrow Unknown

With the drawing of this Love and the voice of this Calling
We shall not cease from exploration
And the end of all our exploring
Will be to arrive where we started
And know the place for the first time.
Through the unknown, unremembered gate . . .

T. S. ELIOT, *LITTLE GIDDING*

Many people across the globe are sensing a powerful urge to let go of the past and yet have no idea of what to let go into. Many of us are realizing that our jobs, our homes, the locations we live in, and our current relationships, no longer reflect who we are. We find ourselves in a paradox. We are not sure where to be or what we want and yet know that we are dissatisfied with our lives. Rather than focusing on what we do not know, it would be more beneficial for us to focus on *what we do know.* What we do know is that our lives no longer seem to fit the person we are becoming. Many of us are finding it impossible to plan for a future. The year 2013 presents to us a blank canvas on which to rewrite the story of our lives.

Since the total solar eclipse of 1999 many people have begun to realize that humanity is in a transitional phase. Many of us have been developing our psychic abilities. Our interest in the paranormal is at an all-time high with books, radio, television shows, movies, and Internet proving to be goldmines of information for raising our consciousness. As we move closer to 2012, we find that everything that relates to our old ways of living is losing significance. Many of our cultural stories, creative art, music, and the media relate to outdated modes of thought and expression. By remaining connected to these old ways we keep ourselves locked into the past and held back from a future bursting with potential. We are being encouraged to live in the *now,* not as a theory or an ideal, but as a reality. The fact is that over millennia humanity has been conditioned to need to *know,* but where has this led us? By living in the *unknown* we can experience liberation from agendas, expectations, and conditioning. We stand on an exciting threshold of uncharted territory.

SUFFERING VERSUS FREEDOM

We are moving from the Age of Pisces into the Age of Aquarius. The Pisces archetype has been teaching us to transcend suffering, to learn forgiveness, to develop compassion, and to love unconditionally. As we continue to move from the Age of Pisces these key areas are brought to our awareness even more. Are we still experiencing suffering? Are we able to forgive with ease and grace? To what degree have we developed compassion? The fact is we attract into our lives the very circumstances that allow us to heal, integrate, and evolve. We have a golden opportunity to take a giant leap forward in 2012. Now is the time to let go of the past and our conditioning and turn toward the future to live a life that uplifts, liberates, and empowers us.

It is vital that we learn to move on and not turn back and look over our shoulder. Humanity has become so accustomed to suffering that we do not realize the extent to which we have become conditioned to it. Suffering has embedded itself deep within our personal and collective psyche. We need to acknowledge that, unconsciously, we have an attachment to it. It is suffering that binds us to the **known,** which has become a refuge for safety, yet it is just that, a place of refuge, not our home. We are afraid to move out of our comfort zones. Our attachment to the known fosters an unhealthy need for security, albeit a false one. We each carry wounds of loss or abandonment. We each carry what psycho-spirituality refers to as the "original wound"—*separation from Source.* This is the core wound that lies at the root of all suffering.

When we are disconnected from God/Source, we are disconnected from ourselves and we experience suffering. Many of us have been raised to believe that Jesus died on the cross for our sins, which further alienates us from God, as we unconsciously battle with the collective guilt of two thousand years. Wars are waged in the name of God, misinterpretations of religion distort the path to God, and laws have been made that have nothing to do with God and everything to do with the manipulation and control of the masses.

Our current world culture is unconsciously addicted to suffering. We are weaned on it, we are educated by it, and we are raised in it. Suffering is all around us, no matter where we go or what we do. We are conditioned to believe that suffering is a natural human state and that we must therefore accept it. Most of what we see, hear, or speak of has suffering woven into it. Modern culture does not realize to what extent it is still immersed in suffering. Once we acknowledge the degree to which suffering permeates *every level of existence* here on the planet, we can consciously choose to remove ourselves from this perpetuating cycle.

Are we not bored with what is on the menu of life? Does the old adage, "familiarity breeds contempt" not apply? Why do modern lives revolve around alcohol, drugs, sex, and money, which mostly serve our escapist tendencies? What are we escaping from? Are these our attempts to avoid suffering? The paradox is that the tactics we use to avoid suffering only result in further entrenching ourselves in an unconscious reality. We limit ourselves to a third-dimensional world, where our altars are our televisions and our main connection to spirit comes through a bottle.

To transcend suffering we need first to acknowledge it is there. To gain an idea of the degree of your own relationship to suffering, pause for a moment and feel your way into the personal and collective suffering around you. Having done so, now make a conscious, focused, and *felt* statement such as, "I acknowledge the presence of suffering within my own conditioned mind-set and in the world around me." This allows you to take the first step toward freedom.

Then let your imagination take you back in time to when suffering might have first begun. You do not need to have a cognitive or intellectual understanding of the history or nature of suffering, you can simply pause and feel, pause and feel, pause and feel, as far back in time as your *felt* memory permits. For a moment, allow yourself to travel back hundreds and thousands of years. Allow yourself to observe momentary flashes of wars and persecutions, the pillaging of the Earth's precious resources, dictatorships, slavery, genocide, and the endless ancestral stories of suffering. Let your imagination observe scene after scene and acknowledge what you are aware of.

All of what you register (and so much more) is tantamount to the amount of suffering that has been held unconsciously within your psyche, for we carry forward what has gone before, not just in our personal ancestrally linked memory, but also in our link to the collective memory. Simply by acknowledging just how much suffering has befallen humanity you can begin to release it from your personal memory and disconnect from the collective memory.

Psychosynthesis (a humanistic and transpersonal psychotherapy) promotes the need to *identify* in order to *dis-identify*. However, we need to revisit the past in a way that does not re-traumatize us, and so induce more suffering, as so often is the case when we share a painful memory. It is vital to our healing to locate a trauma imprint without re-traumatizing ourselves. Then we can effectively begin to heal ourselves of an unconscious addiction to suffering. To accomplish this I encourage the sharing of our stories of trauma in no more than seven to eleven words. By using more than seven to eleven words we can find ourselves becoming re-traumatized, which also affects our biochemistry. Leave out the detail and instead focus on how you feel in the *here and now,* what feelings are alive within you now. So you can say, for example: "I was abandoned as a child," or "I was abused when I was 10." Going into the detail puts us in our heads. Focusing on the feelings allows us to acknowledge, be with, and heal them. *In order to heal, first we must feel.*

Reflecting on the origins of suffering allows us to gain some perspective on the extent to which we are still held in suffering, which in turn keeps us locked into the known. The known is a familiar place built upon our need for security; it is "safe," yet not fulfilling. We experience fulfillment when we feel at one with ourselves, nature, and Spirit. In modern language the term *fulfillment* has developed an entirely different meaning from its true one. We mistakenly associate fulfillment with safety and security.

Fulfillment is a *feeling* of profound proportions. When we know what fulfillment *feels* like, our lives become transformed, as we move into *trust, surrender, gnosis, openness, loving-kindness, forgiveness, compassion, sensitivity, creativity,* and *unconditional love.* When fulfilled, we experience each day as a great adventure, we live in the moment and we are excited by the prospect of the unknown. Fulfillment has nothing to do with security or the known, and everything to do with living in the moment and the unknown.

For modern humanity, true fulfillment is a rare experience. My sense is that the closest most human beings come to fulfillment is when a parent holds a much wanted newborn for the first time, an experience that may fade quite quickly as the demands of the known take hold again. You may believe that you know true fulfillment in moments of intimacy. Is that really true and if so how long does that feeling last? When you are sexually intimate with your partner, do you merge with the cosmos, spirit with spirit, soul with soul, heart with heart, body with body, until no separateness is perceived and there is only Oneness? Such a union is a transcendental experience and allows us to know what true fulfillment really feels like.

Fulfillment is a spiritual experience and any lesser experience may result at best in your being content for a short time and at worst, left feeling empty. We can experience moments of fulfillment through self-love and loving others, or through meditation or creativity, or any experience that engages the heart and calls forth the soul. Security can be bought and paid for, whereas fulfillment is the blessing of a pure and unconditional heart.

We have become addicted to what those in power tell us we need. These are not authentic needs that, when met, restore and empower us, such as a need for love, to express our feelings, to be seen, heard, held, acknowledged, valued, and appreciated. We also have fundamental needs for shelter, food, warmth, and safety. Instead we have adopted pseudo needs that are not our own and are instead the needs of global systems, which—by numbing us to the fact that we are suffering at a personal, collective, and spiritual level—maintain ultimate power and control over our lives while we remain a part of their systems.

T. S. Eliot's "unknown, unremembered gate" leads into the field of dreams. To enable us to stand in that place we are required to trust, surrender, have courage and faith, and live in the moment with neither one foot in the past nor one in the future. The place of the unknown is the dominion of the *Now*. It is the place where we "let go and let God" and where our personal will has aligned with our higher Will. When we arrive at the unknown gate of remembrance, we *remember* who we are and that we no longer need to suffer or to remain locked into the collective pattern of suffering. In the place of the unknown, life effortlessly provides all that we need.

Stepping into the unknown requires total surrender to the path of our hearts and the wisdom of our souls. We need to recognize that we have confused the meaning of safety with security. The first serves our survival needs and the latter our material needs. But what of our spiritual needs? A radical transformation of global, environmental, ecological, social, political, economical, and financial structures is necessary. This becomes a possibility when we reclaim our empowered, authentic selves. If we were to relinquish our personal and collective attachment to suffering, the current dysfunctional global system, which perpetuates suffering, would collapse.

We can learn to live in a different way, one that serves life, each other, nature, and the planet. How can we transcend a history of suffering if we support the very system that keeps it in place? By becoming aware and elevating our consciousness we can break the hold the system has over us. Most people exist in a waking sleep, caught in patterns and routines that keep them secure, yet deeply unfulfilled. By acknowledging this they could change their lives.

It is time to embrace the spirit of adventure that *is* the unknown. We can usher in a new world structure built upon honesty, authenticity, and integrity. Our consciousness is the coal waiting to be fashioned into a diamond. We must let go of both unconscious and conscious attachment to suffering. It can be as simple as flicking a light switch. We need only make up our minds to do so. Suffering belongs in the past. Do not allow it to keep you from your golden future. Be sure to leave suffering behind as you cross the 2012 threshold, through the unknown, unremembered gate that leads to true fulfillment.

In her book *Loving What Is* Byron Katie invites us to ask ourselves four questions regarding what we think we believe. These questions are:

1. Is that true?
2. Can you absolutely know that it's true?
3. How do you react when you think that thought?
4. Who would you be without that thought?

Is it true that suffering is a part of life? Can you absolutely know that suffering is part of your life? Question your belief system. Where did that thought come from? How did you come to believe that? Can you trust the sources that taught you that? What do you believe? How do you react when you tell yourself that suffering is part of life? Just feel what thoughts or feelings arise in you at that thought. Who would you be without the thought that suffering is a part of life? Allow yourself to visualize how you feel without that thought.

WAKING UP

The profound Earth changes, astronomical events, astrological aspects, and the culmination of ancient prophecies, which all converge in 2012, contribute to a higher vibrating quantum field (divine matrix). As a result of this raised frequency, our consciousness and physical bodies are undergoing a transmutation process. We are shifting from duality to unity consciousness. For too long we have been disconnected from the soul, living our lives from a personality level.

The time has come to write a new story for our lives and to let go of those handed down to us by our families and our cultures. These are not our stories; they do not belong to us. We must hand them back with love and write our own. We are being urged to become *aware* and *informed* and, by doing so, to help to educate and prepare others for the transformation of human consciousness in 2012. Both the Earth and humanity are ascending to a higher level of consciousness and evolving to a higher vibrational frequency. The process of ascension will serve to realign the personality with the soul. Ultimately, ascension is about the creation of Heaven on Earth.

Many of us are finding our way to the writings of inspirational new-world thinkers and those at the cutting edge of consciousness. These include Ervin Laszlo, Gregg Braden, Geoff Stray, Alberto Villoldo, Jose Argüelles, Terence McKenna, John Major Jenkins, Daniel Pinchbeck, Sharron Rose, Solara, Celia Fenn, Karen Bishop, Ronna Herman, David Wilcock, Drunvalo Melchizedek, as well as websites such as Worldshift 2012.org, Positive TV, and many other extraordinary sources (see resource directory) that signpost the way ahead in these momentous years leading up to and beyond 2012. Such information helps us to understand why we feel the way we do and guides us in navigating our way through these times of great change and uncertainty.

Collectively, we are living in a time of confusion and anxiety and this is also being experienced at a personal level by many of us. Most of the changes we are experiencing as a result of a consciousness shift are difficult to view as positive or life-enhancing when we feel compelled to end relationships, relocate, leave our jobs, or totally transform our lives. Add to this the physical symptoms and experiences caused by an ascending consciousness and the impact of changing Earth frequencies, and the whole process can feel overwhelming! We may feel that as much as we try to transform our lives to become more peaceful, we often experience upheaval and feel that we are moving backward instead of making progress. This can be because our own frequency is shifting. By responding to this process at an unconscious or conscious level, we invite a period of turbulence as we readjust and realign.

Many of us are feeling tired, lethargic, depressed, confused, and frustrated. Often we find that our attempts to transform our lives appear blocked at every turn. This is a result of a process of realignment to the higher frequencies that now permeate our energetic as well as our physical bodies. In order to move through the tiredness and apathy and motivate ourselves, we must flow with these new higher vibrational energies. By choosing to become informed and aware we can reawaken our passion for life and experience fulfillment. Enormous courage is required to alter our perceptions and embrace the resulting changes in our lives; however, the rewards are immeasurable. Most of us have spent years merely existing, surviving, just getting by day to day, living uninspired lives in which our true selves are barely present. Imagine feeling *alive,* being *in love with life,* and knowing who you are and what you are here for. This is how we are all meant to live.

Most people will avoid change because it usually requires a sacrifice or the need to let go. Change invites us to step out of our comfort zones, which may entail entering into a period of turmoil and upheaval. It may confront us with our deeper fears and a give a sense of going backward, not forward. To use an analogy, the archer draws back the arrow to its furthest point of tension and then simply *lets go*. Pulling the arrow back to its maximum point of tension before releasing it enables it to fly the greatest possible distance. The more we experience upheaval and the bigger the step backward appears to be, the further ahead we will land once we are ready to let go completely and fly.

Believe in yourself. Trust you are being held and guided by the love of those in the heavens who walk with you. Have faith in your unique individuality. Embody a fundamental truth, which is that *you* have something important to offer. Adopt an *attitude of gratitude* for yourself. Trust and surrender are the keys that open the treasure chest of your soul. Believe in *gnosis,* that intuitive felt sense in which *you know without knowing how you know.* Memory, intellect, and academia do not inform gnosis. Gnosis is pure knowing informed only by the heart and soul; it is the highest form of human intelligence. Gnosis engages our intuition, our sense of *feeling* and reveals our true wisdom. Information is power, gnosis is *empowerment.* Too much left brain activity with its emphasis on intellectual and academic information is not conducive for accessing the sixth sense of gnosis. Forget what you think and believe what you *feel*.

Your higher Self is urging you to *let go and let God* and to release all conditioning, belief in struggle, in suffering, and attachment to false security. Start to believe in the magnificence of who you truly are and what your life can offer to those around you and the world you live in.

CHAPTER NINE

The Human Shadow

*If you bring forth what is within you, what you bring forth will
save you. If you do not bring forth what is within you, what you
do not bring forth will destroy you.*

JESUS IN THE GOSPEL OF THOMAS

Our destiny is in our hands. We have the opportunity to become *creators*. Our willingness (or lack thereof) to raise our consciousness and
vibration through healing and integrating our individual (psychological) shadow material will determine whether we collectively rise or fall
as we cross the 2012 threshold. Human consciousness creates waves
of energy that ripple out into the cosmos. If these frequencies are not
conducive to galactic or cosmic vibration and frequency they rebound
directly back to the Earth's astral body (imprinted with the collective
shadow of humanity), and add to the shadow energies already existing
there. In order to clear and heal the Earth's astral body we must first
clear and heal our own shadow.

It is important not to underestimate the way in which our consciousness influences other multidimensional levels and contributes to
the overall frequency of the planet. Your choice to remain unconscious
and uninformed or to become conscious and aware *will* make a difference. Imagine a formation dance troupe whose members must move in

precise synchronization to win the "golden prize." If one, two, or several of the group members decided "I don't need to dance, we'll win anyway," what would happen? This is a good analogy to consider if you believe that as an individual you cannot change anything and think it is best to leave it to others. It is essential to guard against complacency. If your contribution is to only smile or offer kindness to those you encounter, then this is enough for your life to make a difference, because in those moments you are helping to raise not only your own vibration but also the vibration of others.

As a collective, we have a far greater capacity than ever before to create the prophesied "one thousand years of peace." This is because humanity now has an awareness of the concept of a human and collective shadow. Many ancient cultures believed that in a previous golden age people lived in unity and harmony and were fully connected with the higher Self and the light of Spirit. However, part of the evolution of human consciousness has been to experience the opposite of light. It was during the last golden age that the human shadow emerged. This remained unconscious and was the primary cause of the downfall of that once great and golden era.

When there is a split between the personality and the soul, between the ego and the Self, between the human shadow and light, humans project what is held unconsciously outward onto others and onto the world. An example of this can be seen in the contradictory and dysfunctional behavior of those who follow certain religious, philosophical, or spiritual doctrines but who have not explored and healed their own shadow material.

When each person becomes integrated and in harmony with both the inner masculine and feminine, the shadow and the light, the left and right brain, the heart and mind, and the personality and soul, then the reality of a new golden age becomes a possibility. Our capacity to achieve integration to a far greater extent depends on our dedication. We need to ask ourselves why we are in emotional pain and sadness, repression and denial, anger and blame. What do we need to do to heal these feelings? How does it serve us to remain in these emotional states? What's the upside of holding onto them? What's the downside of letting them go?

Many of us have endured unimaginable suffering at the hands of others. How do we move on without splitting off that meaning, repressing or denying it? We must explore and express our feelings with a professional who is skilled enough to hold a space for us and guide us toward freedom from the suffering of the past. Please don't sit alone, talking only with friends, family, or partners about what has happened. This will not solve the deep trauma within. Instead seek support from a professional with whom you feel safe and who you trust with your feelings. (See the resource directory for the type of professional help that can help you to heal the deepest trauma.)

We need to make a choice for something greater, lighter, more inspirational, and more abundant for a golden age to emerge—as we think, so we create. We are poised to enter a new world era, one that offers a blank slate upon which to write a new future. Let us commit to heal ourselves and thus to heal the world.

DESCENSION

If we were already pure love in a bygone golden age, why did we choose to experience anything other than that state?

When I explore this question I am "shown" the keys of a piano. The dark keys represent half notes and the light keys whole notes. There are just twelve notes on the scale, regardless of how many piano keys, and each note is needed in conjunction with the others to create a harmonious or discordant sound. Perhaps these fundamental twelve tones mirror twelve dimensions of human consciousness? My guides show me that the dark keys depend upon the light keys and the light are dependent upon the dark in order to create a perfect harmonic. This speaks to me of the integration of the ego with Self to create the perfect harmonic.

Could it be that the reason for our descent from light into dark is ultimately to serve the universe? Great spiritual masters, philosophers, channels, teachers, and healers have been telling us for millennia that *we are God experiencing itself.* Perhaps we are here to understand that the place of the dark, the shadow, the ego, within each one of us, is as natural as the night. Perhaps we are here to experience this as we do the night, as a place of great peace and stillness, of purity, of mystery, wisdom, magic, and alchemy, of beauty and immense promise? Does the dark, the ego, represent the coal that is a diamond in the making?

Could our existence on the Earth have a more existential meaning than we may have realized? Could it be that we have chosen to lower our vibration and incarnate in the third dimension for the benefit of the higher dimensions from whence we originate? As an analogy, imagine a coal miner who descends into the depths and darkness of the mine to retrieve coal, which can be used to create light and energy, and which has also the potential to transform into a diamond. Is our choice to be here one of courage and altruism? As we cross the 2012 threshold can we now step into the light of a new era?

To answer these questions we need to look more deeply at the relationship between our ego and our higher Self.

EGO AND SELF

The ego is often spoken about as being the worst enemy of the true (higher) Self, yet it is in fact our most loyal friend. The ego is viewed as the enemy because, as adults, it often appears to keep us locked in illusion, powerlessness, lack, the need for security, and self-sabotaging and destructive patterns of behavior. Whenever we make the choice to raise our consciousness and heal our body, mind, and emotions we will encounter the resistance of the ego. The ego is concerned with *survival* and will attempt to overthrow anything that threatens its position.

However, let us not forget the true purpose of the ego and how it serves us. In early childhood, it is the ego that comes to our rescue. As infants, we incarnate as pure soul energy and the higher Self is most present. This true Self is exquisite, undefended, and open. The ego emerges at a point when the Self is not responded to or met in its absolute purity, lovely gentleness, and infinite wisdom. To the child, the world is experienced as a hostile, which is reinforced and reflected through the behavior of its parents, caregivers, teachers, and authorities, as well as the dysfunctional systems of the wider community. It is the ego that shields us from emotional/psychological or actual physical death as infants and children when the harshness and hostility of the world encroaches. We could say that the ego is the warrior who serves the "king" or "queen," the Self that embodies pure unconditional love.

The ego steps in to the role that the Self would have taken had it been able to remain present, instead of retreating due to the harsh, threatening, and hostile environment. Self withdraws, waiting for a time when the consciousness and vibration of the environment is more aligned to its vibration and when it can sense the exact right moment to re-emerge. This does not require that the whole world be in harmony with the Self; it only takes one or more people of like vibration to call it forth. Over the years, the higher Self often remains withdrawn and the ego, which has taken over the life to ensure survival, eventually forgets about the existence of the Self as a result of the layers of defense mechanisms it has put in place. Ego is instinctual, not intuitive, and will *react* instead of *respond*. The ego has a sophisticated set of strategies, which serve as rigid, set programs that keep us locked into *survival mentality*. The ego will continue to create challenging life experiences, which in turn act as a feedback system to the program that is set on "survive, survive, survive."

The ego mistakenly comes to believe that it is the king or queen of the kingdom of the Self. Meanwhile the true regent, the Self, withholds from stepping forward to reclaim its throne until it feels it is safe to do so. Self is pure expression of unconditional love and unity consciousness. Self is all that is good and balanced, integrated and fair, wise and gentle, and evolved and enlightened within each one of us. This never changes, no matter what takes place in our lives. The fourteenth century philosopher Paracelsus said, "Inside each one of us is a special piece of heaven whole and unbroken." Whatever our life circumstances, the Self can be resurrected whenever we feel ready to heal and integrate the ego. Humanity is beginning to move away from suffering consciousness and into a consciousness based upon fulfillment and joy. The Self is the phoenix rising from the ashes of a past that is rapidly falling away to make way for a future of hope and freedom. We could say that the past represents the ego and the future represents the Self.

Ego is driven by fear and it specializes in defense and attack. In psychological terms the ego is regarded as the "adapted" self and the true Self, the "authentic" Self. It is this adapted self that many people believe themselves to be, not aware that there exists another Self, whose essence is pure unconditional love and peace. The extent of our early childhood wounding and the hostility of the early environment are responsible for how disconnected we become from our true Self by the time we reach adulthood. Many of us live active spiritual/religious lives yet remain disconnected from the true Self. This comes as a result of establishing identities that suggest to us that we are "over it," "healed," "above it." Such identities can play the role of defense mechanisms against confronting our excruciating pain/trauma or emotional/psychological wounds from the past. Proof of this can be found in dysfunctional or contradictory conduct or patterns in our personal lives. This does not mean that we are not spiritual, or not in touch with our sublime aspects. But there may be a split between our ego and higher Self. When we are in true alignment, with an integrated ego, we express through the higher Self, which connects us to soul, which gives us access to Spirit.

The first step toward self-healing and self-actualization is to acknowledge the role that the ego has played in our lives so we can appreciate how it has helped us to survive, even if the events we have experienced have caused great suffering. There comes a point on the journey of anyone who is exploring the truth of who they are when the Self begins to prepare for re-emergence. At this stage, the ego becomes aware of the Self. In reaction, the ego devises many defense strategies.

An example is when someone whose heart is closed falls in love. Ego views anything that will awaken the heart as a threat to its survival. Self-sabotaging mechanisms come into operation as the ego begins to defend itself against the emerging Self.

As Self awakens, it begins to communicate with and be influenced by the soul and to access ancient and higher wisdom. As Self begins its journey toward actualization it will encounter ego defenses, as shadow material, which will attempt to block its path. Fear, shame, rage, worthlessness, lack, and pain are some of examples of shadow material. With wisdom and openness, insight and awareness, forgiveness and compassion, empathy and love, Self is able to heal and transmute these shadow energies into its light.

How can we reclaim the throne as the true seat of the Self? If we learn to do this for ourselves and then encourage others to do the same, we can transform a world that currently mirrors the ego to one that reflects the values of the true Self.

EGO AND SELF—A FAIRY TALE

For a moment let us go into our imagination and picture the Self, as a king or queen, returning to reclaim the throne of its kingdom. Let us imagine the many shadow defenses it encounters through the corridors back to the throne room where it will encounter the ego.

Ego has realized that Self is returning to reclaim its kingdom. Symbolically, Ego, experiencing fear and panic, frantically barricades the throne room door. Eventually, Self arrives and knocks on the door, requesting that Ego let it in and relinquish the throne. Ego is defensive, refuses to open the door and prepares to take up arms ready to fight. Ego is prepared to do anything to remain in power and through the closed door tells this to Self. Ego proceeds to try to intimidate Self into submission in the vain hope that Self will scurry away to its place of exile.

However, Self rides the storm whipped up by Ego. Ego feels powerless in the full presence of Self and panics further. What will become of it if Self succeeds in reclaiming the throne? Ego fears it will die. It can see no other outcome. Ego is too afraid to surrender to Self and does not know what to do. Resolutely, Ego digs in its heels and refuses to move. They have reached an impasse. Days, weeks, and months go by with Self remaining present and Ego, locked in the throne room with no resources to maintain its power, becoming weaker. Ego resolves to die on the throne, for surrendering to Self will surely only result in this outcome, until Self throws Ego a lifeline.

Self begins to speak with Ego ever so gently and with great respect. Ego is struck by the tone of unconditional love and compassion in this voice, believing it to be the kindest and most beautiful voice it has ever heard. Ego begins to feel very, very weary, overwhelmed with exhaustion, and begins to pour out its fears to Self, who listens with great compassion and empathy. Ego feels an inexplicable sense of trust as each of its fears are validated by Self. Ego begins to consider the possibility of opening the throne room door, yet again is overcome with fear of the consequences. As much as it wants to trust, for it is so, so tired, it is afraid, believing that Self will betray it. Ego pours out these fears to Self. Self hears Ego's fears and, with the greatest tenderness and compassion, makes a promise. It ensures Ego that its life will be safe and offers a written promise with a golden seal, which stands for absolute integrity and authenticity. Self slides the document under the door for Ego to consider. Ego reads this and notices a separate letter tied with a golden thread. Ego unwraps the letter. It reads:

My dear, dear Ego,

I am so glad to finally have the opportunity to thank you for saving my life. I recognize that without you I would not be here; I would not be alive. You were there when I most needed protecting and even though I have been in exile for all of these years, you ensured that I was provided for. You have held onto my kingdom and many battles you have endured on my behalf. I know you are battered and bruised, scarred and weary, yet you never deserted me or left me exposed, unprotected, or vulnerable when I was unable to return to claim my kingdom. This undertaking has been a great burden for you and it took tremendous courage and strength. How can I ever repay you? What price can be placed on a precious life?

You have served me so very well. You have always been and will remain my hero/heroine and I know that everything you have done was to protect me. I am humbled in your presence for I know that you have suffered greatly in my name. I see the pain and hurt you have endured. I see your heart has been broken. I see the anger and rage you have felt and received. I see the loss you have suffered. I see the loneliness you have endured. I see how you stood in the line of fire for me when the first perceived threat to my existence occurred many years ago and how you have repeatedly done so ever since. All that you have suffered and endured has been to preserve and ensure my existence. You have been the most loyal of friends. You have never abandoned me. You bear the many scars of the trials and ordeals of this life.

My beloved Ego, I have been asleep. For many, many years I was lost in exile. I did not know who I was. During these years I forgot what happened at our first meeting when you shielded me from attack. However, one day, not so long ago, I heard the most pitiful cries of anguish. I heard a voice scream out in the still of the night, "Help me God. Set me free. I can no longer live like this. I am so lonely and in so much pain. I am so tired. Help me someone, release me, from this suffering." That cry awakened me. It was as if I were resurrected as I felt the life force return to me. I heard that cry of anguish, which pierced the very core of my heart. Every cell and fiber of my being heard that call and I recognized that voice as your very own. In that moment I knew that it was now my turn to save you, my dear and loyal Ego.

Ego, I have come once more to be the ruler of my kingdom. I am as new. Even though alone, I have been protected for all of these years and I am unscarred with an unbroken heart.

Dear, dear Ego, would you do me the great honor of being the one to whom I turn to for advice when I need it? Let us once more be friends. I have no need of a wounded ego, yet great need of a healthy one. You no longer need to be lonely for I am here as your friend. First, you must rest and heal. Would you trust me to guide you to the people and situations that can help you to heal, to let go of fear, to learn to play, and to experience joy and love? Will you rest? I have prepared new rooms for you to live in and a beautiful garden of peace and serenity. What say you, Ego?

Ego fell to the floor with great sobs and said to Self "Yes, how very great has been this burden and yet, not a burden, a sacred duty." Ego spoke of the wrong it had done in Self's name, of those it had hurt and how it had hurt itself. Ego hung its head in shame, afraid that by telling the truth of its misdemeanors, Self would abandon it. There was a moment's pause and then Self spoke to Ego in a most compassionate voice saying, "My dear, dear Ego, I love you unconditionally and forgive you; can you forgive yourself? Can you recognize that what you did to others was a result of what had been done to you and even though this does not justify your actions, it does not make you unworthy?"

Ego replied, "Even if I could forgive myself, how will those who I have harmed forgive me? Without their forgiveness how can I truly heal and be free?"

Self replied, "Dearest Ego, you cannot know the karma of those who have crossed your path. Perhaps you were a catalyst or a teacher? You may have brought an experience into someone's life to help them to redress their karma. There is so much that we do not know in this dimension, why punish yourself forever? If you stole from someone, now give to someone or to many. You may give your time or your resources. If you abused someone, help those who have also been abused. If you killed someone, now help others to live. Redress the balance of the actions you regret; for example, where there is fear bring unconditional love.

"Know this Ego, ALL IS FORGIVEN—ALL IS FORGIVEABLE. You only need to forgive yourself and redress your past misdeeds to be free. This is something that you can do everyday. Let it be a joy to do so."

Ego stood up and with great courage and a shaky hand unlocked the throne room door and opened it. Their hearts met before their eyes and in unison they said, "I've missed you friend." From that moment on, a harmonious, positive, and true partnership began. Self took its place upon the throne as ruler of its kingdom, with Ego, now healed, a positive and trusted advisor at its side.

Remember that before we can fully embody the true Self, it is the ego that helps us through the tough times in our life. Once we embrace the true Self we no longer react. Instead we *respond* from the heart, from our *authentic* Self and as a result of this our lives transform. Ultimately, when healing and integrating the ego, we need to first acknowledge its role. The ego deserves our honor and respect, no matter what has gone before, for it very likely saved our life when it first emerged in early childhood. Like any parent, the ego was doing the best it could at the time. Be mindful and recognize that the negative ego needs to heal and retire. The newly emerging positive ego, one that has healed and discovered Self-worth, and is open to give and receive love, gratitude, and appreciation, is a wonderful companion to assist the Self on the journey of the soul.

Be gentle with your ego. Be kind to your ego. Love your ego unconditionally, as the friend and protector it has tried to be and unconditionally love and respect your Self. If you feel that you do not know how to do this, find someone who can remind you, such as an empathic and skilled counselor, therapist, or healer. This in itself is an act of Self-love. (There are contacts in the resource directory at the back of the book that can help to support you to heal and integrate the ego.)

CHAPTER TEN

Raising Consciousness and Vibration

You are in the process of being reformed and refined from the deepest core level. Remember, we have told you that you are no longer moving into the future in linear time/space reality. You are becoming multidimensional and you are moving back in time healing the past as you go forward on the spiral of the future.

ARCHANGEL MICHAEL THROUGH
RONA HERRMAN, JULY 2008

In the early hours of a January morning in 2009, I was awakened by the presence of an angel in my bedroom. This majestic being appeared to be at least twelve feet tall and was violet purple in color. It conveyed to me that it was the "Angel of Elevation." Even though that is not the name it is known by in the heavenly realms, it was the identity it had taken on for those of us on Earth to recognize its message. In a matter of seconds a stream of information was downloaded into my mind, which I have set out below.

The Angel of Elevation told me of the law of elevation and the seven levels of elevated consciousness and how we are moving beyond the universal law of attraction, based on cause and effect and acquisition mentality, and into the law of elevation, founded on higher universal laws that we are now ready to embody. I struggled to grab hold of my notepad and pen and quickly wrote down the information given to me. By the time I looked up the angel had gone. Still, for the rest of that day I felt this angel's continual presence.

In the early hours of the following morning, I was awakened again, but this time there were two angels. One was the Angel of Elevation; the other was a golden angel of equal height, who introduced itself as the "Angel of Unity." It explained that, following the law of elevation, the next level for humanity to aspire to would be the law of unity: whatever affects one, affects all, as ultimately we are all one energy. The law of elevation is part of the new universal knowledge that we need to understand as we approach 2012. The law of unity is the universal law that will begin to take effect from 2013.

The angels requested my assistance to write two books, first about the law of elevation and then, when guided, about the law of unity. For many weeks following the experiences, these angels were with me, guiding my preparation for writing. In the second book, *Beyond 2013: A New Blueprint for an Evolving World,* I shall include the information about the law of unity and the significance of 2013 and beyond. For now, let us focus on the law of elevation as it relates specifically to the raising of consciousness and vibration leading up to 2012.

The law of elevation is powerful and transformative and will support your spiritual unfoldment. If you are able to embrace it, it will raise your frequency, begin to transform your genetic blueprint to a divine blueprint, clear karmic and ancestral patterning, and catalyze the prophesied shift from Homo sapiens to Homo luminous. The first step is to elevate your personal vibration by refining your words, thoughts, and deeds. Next, you need to maintain this raised vibration and then help others to do the same. Finally, you need to support the Earth as she too experiences a shift in frequency. The ability to observe your personal thoughts and conduct *in each moment* is vital if you are to maintain an elevated state of consciousness.

The seven levels of elevated consciousness were given to me as follows:

1. The level of pure unconditional thought, word, and deed
2. The level of pure unconditional self-expression and communication
3. The level of pure unconditional presence and positive regard
4. The level of pure unconditional gratitude and appreciation
5. The level of pure unconditional love and loving-kindness
6. The level of pure unconditional elevated consciousness
7. The level of pure unconditional unity consciousness

The seven levels of elevated consciousness serve as a guide to assist us to raise and maintain a higher vibration. Each one of the levels can be likened to a tuning fork, which harmonizes, realigns, and amplifies our vibration—physically, emotionally, energetically, mentally, psychically, and spiritually. You may find that you are drawn to one level in particular and choose to focus on that before moving on to another level, or find yourself working with several levels simultaneously. By engaging with and fully living the seven levels of elevated consciousness you will begin to radiate magnetic waveform energy and become a positive influence for change.

You may have experienced feeling well and uplifted in the company of certain individuals. This is most probably due to the fact that they vibrate at a higher level than other people in your life. Conversely, if you find others are drawn to you and comment upon how good they feel when in your company, this is because you are vibrating at a higher level and it is quite literally uplifting for them to be in your energetic field. The more you practice and live at these levels the more amplified your vibration will be and the more powerful, positive, and purifying will be the magnetic wave frequency you emit. Most of those whose energy you influence may never know you at a personal level, for they may well be strangers passing by in the street, people convened at a large gathering, such as a music festival or a football match, those you speak with on the telephone, or those who live in or are passing through your neighborhood.

We are bringers of light. It takes just one tiny spark to light the greatest of fires. All contributions are equal, no matter how big or seemingly small. If you do nothing other than to live these levels quietly, you will still be a positive force for change. We urgently need to help raise the human and planetary frequency. We must guide others to *wake up* and remain in this awakened state. For those we encounter along the way, who also feel an urge to unite with the quest for the emergence of a new Earth, we can be role models, helping the light to spread far and wide.

THE ROLE OF THE THREE LEVELS OF THE MIND IN RAISING CONSCIOUSNESS AND VIBRATION

These next few years leading to 2012 are the window of time known as the Quickening, which began at the time of the total solar eclipse of 1999, and peaks in 2012. The term *quickening* reflects the ever-increasing higher vibrating frequencies, and this phase presents to us an opportunity to heal at an accelerated speed. Never before have we had such a varied choice of highly effective healing methodologies available to us. These unprecedented times afford us multiple choices to engage with healing practices that can transform life-denying personal belief systems into life-serving ones.

Changing our minds can heal the world. Gaining some understanding of our internal psychological dynamics and makeup allows us to make more appropriate choices about which healing approach might best support our needs for self-healing. A basic understanding of the structure of the mind not only proves tremendously insightful, but also helps us to understand the enormous influence that the mind has over us. The human mind is made up of three levels: the unconscious, the conscious, and the superconscious.

The Unconscious

I often describe the three aspects of the mind as being like a three-story house, with the unconscious at the lowest level. If we imagine stepping down into the basement of the metaphoric house to visit the unconscious mind, we would be confronted with what would appear to be wall-to-wall machinery with tape recorders and audiovisuals playing a continual stream of every memory, experience, and thought we have ever had.

According to cellular biologist, Bruce Lipton, the unconscious mind is capable of processing *one million* times more information than the conscious mind, handling up to 40 million pieces of data per second. On a day-to-day basis, between ninety-five and ninety-nine percent of our behavioral responses are controlled by the unconscious mind. This often presents a problem because the majority of content stored in the unconscious mind comes from the patterning and conditioning of the people who were around us when we were growing up. In fact, most of the stories we hold at an unconscious level are not even our own. They belong to the generations that have lived before us; they are reenacted by the generations that follow. We are therefore not living our own lives but continuing to recreate the conditioned lives and behaviors of others who formed our unconscious programs. They in turn were preprogrammed by those who raised them. We are generally oblivious to the fact that our behavior is, for the most part, not our own and a lifetime of conditioning and reenactment blinds us to who we really are. Is it any wonder so many of us feel such deep levels of dissatisfaction?

Our early life experiences remain alive in us and reflect to us the lives we now lead. For example, you may have been told you were "not good enough." Taking into account the power of the unconscious mind, you will *unconsciously* set up situations in your life that reflect this as a reality. We unconsciously recreate the *known* because it is "safe" and familiar. Alternatively, if you were told "you are wonderful and perfect just as you are," you are more likely to create a life that is wonderful and perfect just as it is and attract to yourself people who will mirror this inner programming and belief system.

Bruce Lipton refers to the powerful influence of the unconscious by sharing an analogy of someone being given a tape who goes home and puts it in the tape player and presses *Play*. Listening to the tape, they realize they do not like what is playing, so they ask the tape player to play something else; but no matter how much they ask, the machine still plays the same tape. It is not listening. Lipton suggests that instead of pressing the *Play* button, we instead need to press the *Record* button and rewrite the program.

Trauma imprinting occurs when we have experienced something deeply traumatic in our lives, which remains unintegrated, unresolved, and unhealed. Trauma causes us to become stuck in certain stages of our development, with a related story in our unconscious, which then gets projected into our lives. We unconsciously reenact this story, which profoundly influences our life experiences. So, before we can embrace living the seven levels of elevated consciousness, we need to do what we can to eliminate preprogramming, to erase existing negative programs, and re-write new ones.

There are many healing modalities that can assist in shifting unconscious programming and trauma imprints. For example, hypnosis has proven to be exceptionally effective in reprogramming thoughts, feelings, and behavior. Hypnosis allows us to explore the unconscious, to discover hidden psychological, mental, and emotional blocks to health, happiness, and spiritual growth, and then to dislodge them. That in turn can support the eventual clearing of trauma imprints within the aura, as we work to raise our vibration and consciousness. Working with hypnosis can help you to re-record outdated tapes and set new programs in place to influence your conscious mind.

The Conscious Mind

Returning to our metaphor of a house, the conscious mind is found on the ground level, which is where we tend to conduct our lives. The conscious mind consists of a series of data processors, which filter, interpret, and act upon the information received from both the unconscious and superconscious minds. The ground level is wired up to the basement and receives much of its life-guiding information through this wiring. As a result, life continues to be lived in a certain way, a safe and known way, as dictated by the tapes running in the basement. The unconscious also stores valuable information, which can guide us to make choices that are life-serving and life-saving too.

In essence, the conscious mind is a creative mind. It is where we experience free will and have the ability to say "enough." The conscious mind is able to rewrite the programs in the unconscious mind when needed. The conscious mind also serves as a bridge between the unconscious and superconscious.

The Superconscious Mind

The superconscious mind is found on the top floor of our symbolic house. This is a sacred space, vast, pure, and light. This is the floor where our most sacred valuables (values) are stored. The superconscious is the seat of the soul and the soul is *imagination in action*. If you wish to know how to have a stronger connection with your soul, engage your imagination: meditate, write, design, paint, sing, dance, involve and envelop yourself in creativity.

The superconscious is the level of our direct link to divine inspiration and our connection to higher-dimensional realms. It is the place where the wisdom of the higher Self can be accessed to help clear the unconscious mind of the discordant patterns and energies found continually whirring on the playing tapes. These unconscious messages, which have become deeply ingrained, prevent us from rising to our full potential and living our true purpose.

The superconscious also has wires that extend to the data processors found on the ground floor of our metaphorical house, which represents the conscious mind. When they are disconnected, the conscious mind is denied the exalted insights and wisdom from the superconscious mind. When they are connected, however, we are given access to whole new dimensions of ourselves. They enrich, inform, and enlighten the conscious mind, which serves as a channel for these more soulful offerings. It is the superconscious that reveals the higher purpose of the soul.

Hypnosis can be a gateway for accessing your superconscious, a much under-explored potential powerhouse for healing, transformation, and transcendence. It is interesting to note that the word *hypnosis* contains the word *nosis*. Gnosis is the voice of the superconscious mind. By working with the unconscious, via hypnosis, we can release negative life-denying patterns and replace them instead with new positive life-serving ones. Hypnosis bypasses the conscious, rational mind and engages us instead with the abstract mind where we can access past and future lives, extradimensional contact, hypercommunication, creativity, will, and spiritual power. We can cultivate a mind where we can embrace a life that is devoid of fear and rooted in love and trust. This is the life we are truly meant to be living with all three levels of the mind in unity.

THE POWER OF SOUND
IN RAISING CONSCIOUSNESS

There are many other healing modalities available that may support our return to well-being and wholeness. However, if we are not living and acting from love we will find it impossible to reach inner balance and peace. For us to succeed in ascending, transcending, elevating, and raising our consciousness and vibration we need to reside within love. The time has come for us to realize the power of love and the immeasurably beneficial and healing effect that sound can have on our well-being and consciousness. Sound and waveform experts have shown that the energy of love creates a vibration that appears as a long, coherent waveform, which interacts and intertwines with our DNA helixes to re-encode and bring about measurable vibrational shifts within our energy field. One experiment showed that when an unbraided DNA strand was exposed to the vibration of love, the strand spontaneously recoiled itself. Fear, on the other hand, forms a short, incoherent waveform, which inhibits re-encoding and frequency shifts.

We need to choose carefully the sounds we listen to because of the impact that they have on us. When we listen to "feeling" music, which evokes an emotion within us, the autonomic nervous system, respiration, blood pressure, pulse rate, and galvanic skin responses are affected. The heart rate is sensitive to volume and rhythm. Sound has the capacity to trigger the response of love or fear. Think about the use of "creepy" music in paranormal programs or horror films, which has the specific purpose of inducing fear. Contrast this with hearing music that is poignant and beautiful. These waveforms can be likened to a potent healing balm and our multi-leveled selves respond by expanding, opening, and being healed. Sound waves that are loving open the heart and engage the right brain, allowing expansion and supporting us in our quest to cultivate an inner state of peace. Harsh or "creepy" sounds produce fear, activate the left brain, and disconnect us from the heart.

Noise pollution is as detrimental to our health as air pollution. Traffic on the streets, building construction, roadwork, and other unnatural sounds are experienced by us as stress. The sounds of what we love, such as bird song, land animals, the ocean, the gentle rush of the wind, laughter, and so on are all good medicine for the soul.

Discernment is a wise approach when choosing the company we keep. The presence of another can have a startling effect on our vibration by either raising it, lowering it, or synchronizing. If you take two tuning forks, strike one, and bring it near to the other, the second will automatically synchronize to the same frequency. Similarly, another person's energy field and vibration can affect you for better or worse. Think about those with whom you share your life. You will know if your frequency is raised or lowered depending on who you are with. Do you feel uplifted or drained? Does your mood alter when you spend time around certain individuals or groups?

Places hold a vibration too. How do you feel in your neighborhood? A town? A city? A sacred site? Everything is energy—people, places, nature, animals, buildings, towns, cities, holy places—everything. Part of the ascension process is to be discerning. Prioritize feeling radiant, uplifted, joyful, loving, creative, loved, accepted, visible, valued, respected, and celebrated, for this will truly raise your vibration and elevate your consciousness.

The Healing Power of Language

Spiritual teachers and advanced ancient civilizations have long been teaching us that we are subtly or overtly impacted by words, sounds, and energy. Recently a team of Russian researchers, led by Russian biophysicist and molecular biologist Pjotr Garjajev, have proved this to be true. They have joined with linguists and geneticists in a venture to explore the ninety percent of "junk" DNA that is separate from the ten percent currently used to build proteins. They have been working on techniques using radio and light frequencies to repair genetic defects, such as chromosomes that have been damaged by X-rays. Their results are revolutionary. They have proved that DNA can be influenced and reprogrammed simply by using words and frequencies. This eliminates the need to cut out and re-introduce single genes from the DNA, which is the approach used by Western scientists.

According to Garjajev and his team, our DNA serves to store data and is also an advanced communications system. They have shown that the alkalines of our DNA follow a regular grammar and have set rules, like human languages. This reveals that human language is not a coincidence, but is in fact a reflection of our DNA. As the basic structure of DNA-alkaline pairs and language are the same, we can also use words and sentences in the human language to reprogram our DNA. As long as the appropriate frequencies are used, living DNA will always respond to language-modulated laser and radio waves.

The DNA response to language is wholly natural and stands to prove that techniques such as affirmations, mantras, hypnosis, and so forth can and do alter human consciousness and have an impact on our physical experiences. However, for this to occur with maximum success the frequency has to be correct. To establish a conscious communication with our DNA requires that we work on our inner process. A certain level of emotional, psychological, and spiritual maturity is required to enable us to do so. The more developed and conscious we are of how we use language and sound, the more our genetic blueprint will align with our divine blueprint. Marshall Rosenberg, Ph.D., refers to Nonviolent

Communication (NVC) as "The lost language of humankind." (See resource directory.)

Sound Healing

The Earth changes taking place and the increase in the intensity of cosmic vibrational influences are producing actual physical responses in our bodies and in the Earth. To help ourselves and our planet we can support these changes within our vibratory fields by engaging in certain activities. Sound travels in a waveform. Waves are measured as cycles and sound is measured in cycles per second. This is called its *frequency*. Slow waves result in slow vibrations and accelerated waves create fast vibrations. Every organ, cell, bone, tissue, and system within the physical body is in a constant state of vibration. By absorbing certain frequencies, through music and sound, we can raise our vibration and so align with the new energies and frequencies entering the Earth and our own bodies. Music, sound, and vocal harmonics powerfully assist us to raise our vibration and maintain it at a higher level.

A new genre of music and sound has emerged since the late 1980s, known as "vibrational sound and wave form energy music." It is becoming internationally recognized as an effective way of healing and raising our vibration and consciousness; it can also alter our DNA structure. This is not the first time humans have recognized the powerfully transformative effects of sound for creating altered states of consciousness, deep healing, and an upgrading of human frequency. Sound has been used in these ways since prehistoric times by shamans (persons with the ability to contact and see other worlds and dimensions) and medicine people from different cultures around the world. Chanting, drumming, and replications of the sounds of nature, which are the origins of all music, have influenced humanity since our early beginnings when we lived in harmony with the Earth.

In those earlier times merging with the Earth and the heavens was as natural to us as breathing. We were aligned with the Earth's frequency and journeying to other realities and dimensions was an accepted part of our lives. We discovered how to create instruments and use our voices to mimic the sounds of nature. We exposed ourselves to new waveforms as we created basic sound tools, including whistling vessels, which resulted in early psychoacoustic effects. These primal sound enhancers were fashioned from natural resources and created new sound frequencies, which enhanced communication with and travel to higher-dimensional realms.

Ancient Peruvian mummies were found buried with pipe-like instruments. When these implements were first discovered they were thought to be water jars. However, when blown into, they were found to create powerful psychoacoustic effects. Recent experiment and research has shown that the entire cranium of a person blowing into one of these whistle-type instruments acts as a resonating chamber, an effect that cannot be reproduced on a recording. These whistles were used to create altered states of consciousness via the low frequency sounds produced by the interaction of the higher notes. It has been discovered that these complex instruments played a key role in the lives of the Incas and Maya.

We are wired for the healing influence of sound. Just as walking, especially barefoot, stimulates our organs and body systems without our registering it at a conscious level, specific auditory experiences rebalance us. Psychoacoustic researchers suggest that sound, particularly vocal harmonics, triggers different brain chemicals, including melatonin (note how the word *tonin* is contained within the word melatonin). Sound harmonics—which include the use of crystal singing bowls, Tibetan bowls, tuning forks, and vocal harmonics, as practiced through toning, chanting, and the use of mantras—stimulate different portions of the brain and create new neural synaptic connections. This opens us to the possibility of experiencing a unique deep healing.

Jonathan Goldman, a pioneering sound expert who introduced the concept of *resonant frequency healing,* tells us that the correct frequency (the actual sound being used) is most important but equally so is the *intent* we hold in order to bring about overt or subtle healing experiences. By *consciously* working with these new wave form sounds, while at the same time focusing our awareness on a specific intent, we can effect great changes within our physical and energetic bodies.

It is interesting to note that a thirteenth tone has only recently been discovered by pioneers at the cutting edge of sound research. Perhaps it imprints the presence of a thirteenth dimension into our consciousness. Evidence has yet to be found of this thirteenth tone existing in any music anywhere in the world. These pioneers are currently experimenting with the possibilities of using this thirteenth tone for healing.

The Voice as an Instrument for Healing and Ascension
Reclaiming the True Voice

The voice is a primary instrument. There was the voice in the beginning, which at that time expressed as a sound. We have come a long way since our primitive roots and can now express our "sound" as melodically as a gentle harp, piano, acoustic guitar, violin, or flute. We do not have to be prolific singers for our voice to be experienced by others as beautiful. There are many people who feel they are not able to sing but have a beautiful speaking voice. Conversely, the voice can be experienced as a cacophony of musical instruments played disharmoniously or at great speed. It may jar, unnerve, and add to any tension we are feeling without our conscious recognition that it is contributing to our stressful state. Such a voice can also make others feel unbalanced or ill.

Take a moment to think about how you express yourself in words and sound. How would you describe your voice? Are you soft-spoken? Is your voice melodic? Have you been told your voice has a healing quality? Is your voice calming and gentle? Is it measured? Perhaps you speak very quickly? Is your voice commanding, strong, and assertive? Is it a meek, apologetic voice? Is it loud, shrill, or booming? Do you say very little or are you prone to talk incessantly? Does your voice convey tension? What pitch is your voice? Does it sound nasal and pinched? Where in the body does it come from? Does it rise from your throat? Your heart? Your belly?

Most of us do not realize or give a second thought to what our voice says about us. We may not realize that our voice reveals our inner state of being. The voice is a vibrational sound resonant frequency. Its sound conveys far more information to us than the words that are being expressed. When we are disconnected from our true and authentic Self, we adopt a "pseudo-voice," the voice of the ego, which is not representative of who we truly are. The language and tone of voice used by some adults is often representative of a young girl or boy, revealing unhealed childhood trauma.

The language we use to express ourselves is also a vibrational sound resonant frequency, which affects not only our own vibration but also that of our immediate environment. Dr. Masaru Emoto's work, documented in his book, *The Hidden Messages in Water,* is proof of this. He conducted thousands of experiments in which he and his team directed harsh, unkind, and negative words, or loving, kind, and compassionate words to water samples. Using a special technique, he photographed the water molecules before and after exposure. Every sample that had negative thoughts or words conveyed to it formed broken, fractured, murky crystals, and every sample exposed to loving thoughts and words formed beautifully structured light-filled crystals.

Dr. Emoto experimented with different voice tones, languages, even expletives, and pasted kind or unkind words onto sample bottles of water. Each time, the results were the same. Stunning crystal formations appeared when kind words were conveyed, and broken, dark crystals formed when harsh words were used. As humans are 90 percent water, this astonishing research shows us how our physical health and well-being are affected by our thoughts and words. Dr. Emoto's research reveals how we can alter our own crystalline aqua-system to one of beautiful, light, fully structured crystals or a mass of dark, unstructured, fragmented, broken crystals.

One of the most powerful healing tools we are naturally blessed with is our voice. If you wish to take a giant leap forward in your ascension process, begin by transforming your voice and changing your choice of language. Recognize the impact of words and thoughts on the physical, emotional, mental, and etheric bodies and how these can either activate or deactivate the light-body. Our thoughts, voice, and language need to be in alignment with and represent the essence of who we are, the soul Self, if we are to notice extraordinary changes occurring within ourselves and our lives. Years of struggle, pain, and sadness have robbed us of our true sound. This authentic sound is what we need to reclaim in our quest for healing and wholeness. As we begin to reconnect with our core essence, we start to align with our true voice, which is often lighter and richer, and has the ability to soothe and calm all who hear it. Our true voice helps us to harmonize our chakras, elevate our consciousness, raise our vibration, and attract extraordinary experiences.

Observe people who are an inspiration to the world and you will notice that most of them will speak with gentleness, grace, humility, and a quiet confidence. Humanitarian role models, including the Dalai Lama, Mother Teresa, and Gandhi, have been noted for speaking softly with love, grace, and compassion. The Essenes taught their young to speak gently. It is reported that Jesus, himself believed to have been an Essene, had a calm and soft voice. Tibetan children are also taught to speak with a gentle voice as part of the respect for all life that is woven into their upbringing. This is a reflection of their culture.

When we listen to the voices of the heroes and heroines or lead actors and actresses in films, they nearly always speak in soft masculine or feminine tones. Unconsciously, we respond to these tones. Such voices add weight to the authenticity, intelligence, or vulnerability of the characters and suggest to us that they are fundamentally trustworthy. Examples of this include silver screen characters such as Balian in *Kingdom of Heaven* and Aragorn and Arwen in *The Lord of the Rings*. In contrast, characters who are portrayed as dysfunctional use a tone that is coarse, rough, or high pitched. In life, we have as long as we need to sum up the character of a person, but on film this has to be established in seconds. The voice provides the information the viewer needs in order to make a connection with and assessment of the lead characters and to follow the story.

In the quest to raise our vibration and alter our consciousness we can use the voice as an instrument and as a powerful healing tool. With only a little training or attention your voice will lead you to the exact frequencies necessary to experience healing and transformation. In meditation we slow our energy, pulse, heart rate, and mind with intention and breath. We can do the same with our voice. However your voice sounds now, you can alter its pitch, tone, and resonance to make it gentle, strong, quietly confident, calm, and present.

Each one of us has had an experience of our true voice. Think of a time when you felt an intense wave of love and remember the tone of your voice in that moment. It was almost certainly softer, as in that moment your heart and true Self, not your mind or ego, was expressed through your voice. Recall for a moment *how that feels*. Feel that feeling in your body—it is so nourishing and healing. We speak in this manner when communicating with babies and young children, when in union with our love, or when we encounter an animal we feel an affinity with. Remember how your voice changes when you are expressing condolences at the news of someone's passing or when you share concern for someone who is ill or is experiencing difficulties. The tone and pace with which you speak in such moments is closer to the voice of your heart and is your true voice.

The Transformative, Transcendental Sounds of AH, OM, HU

Jonathan Goldman speaks of the transformative and healing power of "planetary healing sounds" and mantras and encourages us to chant the sounds "AH," "OM," and "HU." He refers to the AH sound as a "sacred seed syllable" and as the generator of peace and compassion. He points out that many great spiritual teachers names contained AH, including Yeshua, Buddha, Krishna, as well as invocations such as Hallelujah and Amen. AH is said to be the sound of the heart and is perhaps the original energetic intent behind art—to connect us with the heart. AH is the first sound we make when we enter the world and usually our final sound as we depart.

Across the planet, OM is the sacred sound most often chanted. OM is thought to be the most sacred of chants, dating back thousands of years. OM is said to create a bridge to the spiritual dimensions where we can experience contact with higher-dimensional beings. The sound of OM is associated with peace.

The Sufi believe that the sound HU is the oldest sound mantra in existence and consider HU to be the highest vibrating mantra. The sound of HU is believed to lead to transcendence, enlightenment, and Oneness with Source. HU is said to have an extraordinary, transformative, clearing, and balancing effect on the human being and is believed to activate and link together the crown and the heart chakras.

If you would like to experiment with the transformative effects of sound to support the ascension process, be wise and cautious in your approach, for exposure to a varied range of frequencies in concentrated forms can overstimulate the hypothalamus, pituitary, and pineal centers of the brain. Little is known of the long term effects of exposure to such frequencies. Everything in moderation is an important consideration, as overexposure can be dangerous for a novice and has the potential to bring on premature strokes or other brain imbalances. You may wish to approach a professional sound healer who can expertly guide you into sound wave transformational healing experience. If not, take small steps in your own experiments and build upon these small steps over a lengthy period of time.

Purchase only published works from experts in the field. Much is now available in CD format. Seek out works from reputable psychoacoustic researchers including: Joseph Puelo, Leonard Horowitz, Jonathan Goldman, Robert Monroe, and Tom Kenyon, all of whom are at the cutting edge of resonant frequency healing and whose published works are recognized. By listening to the works of these pioneers, you have an opportunity to work with sound and bring about changes within your vibratory field and your brain and body chemistry to aid your healing and ascension process.

CHAPTER ELEVEN

Creating a Home for Higher Consciousness

Love begins at home, and it is not how much we do . . . but how much love we put in that action.

MOTHER TERESA

Our homes can either raise or lower our vibration, which can have an impact on our consciousness. One of the greatest antidotes and medicines for stress, anxiety, and illness is a peaceful home. It can be a caravan, a yurt, a tipi, a mobile home, a room in a nursing home, a flat, a terraced house, a barn conversion, or a "chocolate box" cottage. Remember, it is not the outer wrapping, but what is on the inside that counts. To manifest a home that is tranquil and calming is simply a choice.

Sometimes we are lucky enough to be taken to somewhere beautiful and sometimes we are guided to where we need to be for our soul growth or because our energy is needed there. Although we may choose to live in a busy environment because our higher purpose calls on us to be in such a location, we can still create a sanctuary of calm and peace within our home, a place to nourish, heal, and uplift us and those who visit us.

Take some time to consider any manageable changes that you would like to make in terms of décor and layout. You do not need to rebuild it! Sometimes just redecorating or adding some new soft furnishings or a few candles and gentle lighting is enough to facilitate a shift of feelings and bring a sense of peace into the home.

Remember, *as we think so we create*. So a good place to start with any desired changes is in the imagination. This sows the seed of intent and sets into motion the energy of what you wish to change, which in turn can manifest as a reality. Allow yourself to imagine a home that is filled with peace and then begin to make that possible.

Try answering a few questions as you take an honest look around your home. Allow yourself to acknowledge what you may have been turning a blind eye to for some time. You may like to write down or simply make a mental note of the feelings and sensations you become aware of when focusing on your home environment.

How would you describe your home?
- What do you see?
- How does it make you feel?
- What do you need more of?
- What do you need less of?
- What is perfect?
- What is uplifting?
- Which are your favorite rooms? Why?
- Which are your least favorite rooms? Why?
- Is it a place of peace, serenity, tranquility, clarity, passion, positivity, creativity, stillness, nourishment, sustenance, nurture, sanctuary, love, soul, balance, light, and Spirit? Or does it represent lack, chaos, confusion, darkness, control, negativity, pain, sadness, hurt, noise, imbalance, and a lack of spiritual presence? Does it lack soul?

Now take a look at your outer environment. Again, you might like to write down or simply make a mental note of the feelings and sensations you notice when focusing your awareness there.

Take a look at your outer environment.

- How do you *feel* when you focus your attention on your outer environment?
- What is happening out there?
- What do you hear?
- What do you see?
- How important is it to you that you have access to what is outside your front door, just around the corner, or further down the road?
- Is there anything that you find discordant, jarring, or stressful about the environment in which you live?
- Is it a busy environment?
- Is it noisy?
- Is there peace and stillness?
- Is there space to breathe?
- Are you comfortable in your environment?
- Does it make you feel alive?
- Do you dream of getting away from your outer environment and going somewhere completely different?
- Is the environment you live in ideal for you?
- If not, why is that, and where is?
- What do you need to do in order to manifest your ideal environment?

CREATING AN UPLIFTING HOME

Creating balance within the home is uplifting and inspiring and requires little effort or expense. Notice the color of the walls, the flooring, the soft furnishings. Do they invoke a sense of peace, abundance, and an uplifting spiritual energy? What kind of objects do you have around you? Are they dust collectors that fill a gap or objects that have a sacred meaning for you?

You can change the energy of your home to make it look and feel dramatically different, which in turn will make a difference to you. It is amazing the difference a bit of paint and a different colored floor can make. To raise the vibration of your home choose light, uplifting colors, perhaps white with a hint of gold or pastel colors on the walls. Magnolia is an excellent neutral color and when the Sun shines it imbues a beautiful gold light in the room, or you can buy uplighters with low-wattage energy-saving bulbs to cast a similar light into the room.

Maintain a shoes-off policy so that you can enjoy lighter colors on some of your floors. If you have floorboards you can paint them white, rustic, or teal colors or you can varnish them. If you have a threadbare dark or bland colored carpet you can replace it with a color that you find uplifting, even if it is only possible to do so in one room or to cover it with large rustic rugs. You can pick up some great bargains in the free ads if budget is an issue.

Get some big cushions or comfy soft sofas, the type that hug you when you sit on them (again the free ads can be invaluable when choosing quality furnishings at affordable prices). Have a smoke-free policy in the home; visitors really do not mind standing outside to smoke. Burn blends of organic oils, like geranium, lavender, ylang ylang, neroli, or bergamot in an oil burner, or burn some natural incense like Nag Champa.

Hang white or brightly colored muslin (very affordable) to frame windows or doors. Invest in some lovely colored throws (these can be found in markets, shops, or again the free ads) that you can drape over the sofas and beds to bring an uplifting energy into the home.

Always have a vase of fresh flowers. You deserve to buy yourself flowers regularly, even if it is a simple posy, and dot a few potted plants around to bring some "live" energy into the home. If you have an old fireplace, this is a great place for an altar, or if it is working, make a crackling fire for relaxation and gazing into as you allow your imagination to flow freely. You can create a similar feeling by spreading a few candles around the room you spend time in; however, ensure they are on a protective surface and away from billowing curtains or anything that could catch fire should they fall. Remember to never leave lighted candles unattended.

Be mindful of the music you play. Music can raise or lower the vibration in a room. If you have a sunny window hang a large clear crystal in it so rainbows dance around the room when the Sun shines or hang some beautiful colored stained glass window hangings. Buy some *static* fairy lights in classic and rainbow colors for long, dark dreary days or relaxing nights as they help to lift the atmosphere and bring a sense of magic into the space. Treat yourself to a special candle, one that is organic, natural, and fills the room with a beautiful aromatherapy scent. You can create an altar in every room or a special place in the room, where you can light your candle and place it near photographs or beautiful images, words of inspiration, crystals, or any other objects that are sacred to you.

Creating a Sanctuary

Creating a place of peace within the home is an excellent remedy for stress, illness, and tiredness; spending time in such a space can be like a balm for the soul, healing us and bringing us peace from the inside out. Even if initially you have only one room in the house for this, it is a good place to start. A dear friend of mine has a house in which all of her "spiritual" objects were kept within one room on the top floor, away from the eyes (or potential judgments) of visitors. We were both aware that what lay at the root of this was a past-life memory, one in which she wielded a great deal of spiritual power. By her own discovery, she had come to realize how she had abused that power. For many years, she had struggled with her spiritual and religious beliefs, aware of a deep connection with a higher source, which brought great peace and comfort, yet at the same time feeling very uncomfortable and at odds with it.

After much inner exploration she was able to find a place of peace with her spirituality and felt ready to decorate the rest of her house with beautiful crystals, candles, meaningful art, spiritual objects, and to burn incense and oils and play meditation music. She was no longer afraid to show this part of herself to others for fear of being judged, because she no longer judged herself or feared her spirituality. Her readiness to spread her spirituality throughout her home for all to see confirmed to her that the deep past-life wound she had carried had finally healed. However, her first step of acknowledging her shaky connection to Spirit was that of setting aside one room to find peace and connect with her spiritual Self. So, if you find yourself a little concerned about beginning to transform your home into a sanctuary of peace, find a manageable starting point, even if it is a windowsill or a corner of your bedroom. Just having one sacred object somewhere near to you can bring a sense of peace.

Just setting up an altar can bring an immediate sense of the sacred and peaceful into your home. All you need to do is to choose a specific area in a room. It could be a corner, the center of the room, or a windowsill. An altar can be created by simply placing some fresh flowers upon it. You can add pictures of Jesus, Buddha, angels, the Dalai Lama, Mohammed, or other great spiritual beings. You could also include crystals, candles, incense, herbs, resins, or anything else that has significance and meaning for you, such as a feather you came across while walking or something someone has given to you that has great emotional or spiritual value. None of what you place on your altar needs to have material or religious value, only heart value.

LOOKING INTO THE MIRROR
OF YOUR HOME AND ENVIRONMENT

We can neglect our homes or turn them into our personal version of a palace, the latter not being at all dependant on material wealth. The body is said to be the temple of the soul and your relationship with your home says much about how you care for your body. Someone who is obsessive and needs to control the cleanliness and upkeep within their home is not necessarily someone who has a harmonious relationship with their body. Often those who create these types of homes feel unwell and are thrown off balance if anything is moved from its designated place. For those who live in or visit such homes this can be an uneasy experience, which says more about the psychological condition of the host than the visitor. Those who are relaxed and calm tend to have a calm and beautiful home, one in which you feel comfortable and at ease.

Your home and environment can offer valuable insights into how you feel about yourself and your life, if you care to explore what they mirror to you. Every room of your home says something about you, your psychology, about how you feel and your values. If you look at your home from a psychological or spiritual perspective it can show those places within you that may be in need of some attention and healing. The rooms where we feel loved and peaceful highlight those places that are alive within us.

The outer environment around your home also tends to indicate much about your "inner" landscape—how you feel inside. It does not necessarily reflect your spiritual development (although in many cases it can). However, it will say something about how aligned and balanced you are personally with your outer life. If your home is chaotic and yet your outer environment is peaceful and surrounded by nature this indicates something about you, just as if your home is a haven of peace, yet the outer environment is chaotic.

Let us imagine that you live on a beautiful island, yet your home is disorganized, cluttered, and messy. This may reveal an imbalance between your soul, represented by the peace and nature of island life, and your personality/ego self as represented by your home. On the other hand, your house may be a haven of peace, while the immediate external environment might be one of chaos, noise, and pollution. This may be indicative of someone who is deeply spiritual or heart-centered yet has to don a mask each time she steps out of her front door, in order to manage the external environment. So the world sees only an adapted version. However, in her personal life such a person is able to remove the mask and reveal her authentic self. In either case there is a discrepancy between the outer and inner.

The locations and homes that we live in can indicate where there is a psychological and spiritual imbalance within the Self. Many people are actively spiritual and yet feel their lives are out of control. They feel unhappy, unfulfilled, or live in a state of lack, all of which is mirrored by the home. It is possible to be integrated and whole and live in a busy environment, yet, more often than not, such people regularly visit the countryside or coast to "ground," breathe, and recharge before once again entering an unnatural environment such as a busy town or city.

☽ A Look in the Mirror

1. Connect to your home for a moment. Just picture the layout of each room and how it makes you *feel*. Think of three words that describe how you *feel* about your home. Trust your initial response and accept the words that come. If you find more arise, accept these too. Write the words down.

2. Now do the same for your environment. Reflect on what is outside of your home. Scan the environment and then note the first three words that arise in your mind. Again, trust your initial responses and accept these. Make a written note of the words. What you have jotted down reveals certain aspects about yourself and is a great way of understanding how you feel. These words are a mirror for you at this stage of your life and can offer you clues about where you need to focus your awareness and what you may need to do next.

3. Now ask yourself "How would I describe my home?" Write that down and then acknowledge how these words describe aspects of yourself. Add your own insights of what your home represents to you and then turn those insights around to reveal insights about your life or yourself at a deeper level.

4. Now ask "How would I describe my wider environment?" Write down your initial response and notice how your response

indicates how you may feel when you focus your attention on yourself.

5. Now ask "What is happening out there?" Write down your initial response. This may give you a clue as to what is happening inside yourself.

PEACE IN THE COUNTRY, PEACE IN THE CITY

With regard to the locations in which we live, we may feel we have no choice, but there is always a choice. We may choose to live on an estate in a quiet country town as opposed to a busy, polluted city. Or we can choose to live in a busy city and yet feel deeply peaceful, with a sense of meaning and purpose to our lives through an active vocation. The fact remains that no matter where you live, you can make your home a sanctuary. It can be a place to nourish, heal, and uplift you and those who visit you. In recent years I have rented some beautiful inexpensive places set in stunning environments. Many years ago, however, I lived in one particular house set in the middle of a car lot in West London. Visitors would be shocked when they drove into the car lot, as it was the last place they expected to find me! Yet, when they stepped through my front door they would be enchanted by what they found, a place that immediately calmed and soothed. My home became likened to a healing sanctuary and the preferred meeting place for friends. Many a joke was made when people arrived at the car lot and then entered my house. So there can be a discrepancy between the outer and inner when we find ourselves located in particular places where life takes us for specific reasons. However, I recognize how the noise and pollution of the outer environment mirrored my own healing edges at that time.

To move to a preferred location might mean that we have to reorganize our lives to make it possible to live in such an environment. To follow our hearts takes courage and commitment. When we listen to the heart it acts like a compass and will always steer us in the right direction. If we really desire to live in nature we must be prepared to make a dramatic decision about our existing lifestyles and be willing to undergo radical changes. Let us say that somebody has a secure nine to five job and lives on a busy road in a town or city, yet longs to live in the countryside. It is a matter of courage and takes trust to make the choice to turn that dream into a reality. This is when we must listen to the heart. A rural cottage can cost less whether bought or rented than a house in a city. We can find ways to earn an income even if we live rural—where there's a will there's a way!

When we reach a point of choosing an experience of a different home life, it is usually because our priorities are changing. Acting on this can result in a wonderful life change. While this may cause a dramatic fall in our financial security, such a move can be beyond value at a physical, emotional, mental, psychological, energetic, and spiritual level. To walk in nature; to hear the rush of the river; to breathe fresh air; to see the green of nature, the gold of sand, the turquoise seas; to taste the salt of the ocean in the air or hear the full chorus of bird song are phenomenological experiences—that is, they engage all our senses. We are by nature sensory beings and when all the senses are active, we feel alive. Such a lifestyle choice far outweighs the cutbacks that may be necessary to move from a city to the countryside.

We have become accustomed to high maintenance lifestyles. But creating a sustainable life, although presenting an initial challenge, can prove to reconnect us to fundamental values and enable us to meet primary needs. These needs can be more fully met in nature and community living, as we interact more with the land and with our neighbors in our commitment to a sustainable lifestyle. This may come about by bartering—exchanging eggs for kindling, for example.

Reverend Peter Owen-Jones, an English Anglican clergyman, author, and television presenter has recently embarked upon a lifestyle experiment to live sustainably, without money. His experiences have been documented in a three-part television series titled *How to Live a Simple Life,* in which he commits to experiencing life freed from material constraints. Inspired by St. Francis of Assisi, who lived spiritual values without money, he says the idea for *How to Live a Simple Life* came to him in 2008, as he watched the banking system crumble around the world. "It was just after the credit crunch hit," he says. "I remember thinking, 'This is insane. We're facing this massive meltdown and we're all being asked to spend money. There's something unwell here.'"

There are those who find themselves compelled to live in a city after many years of living in the country or on the coast. As long as they recreate the peace found in a country or coastal setting within their homes, by using pictures, colors, plants, flowers, water features, and nature sounds, and so on, they can maintain inner balance and harmony. It is not so easy to live sustainably in a town or a city, as doing so requires us to reconnect with nature and community. I recall being in London with a friend who was trying to track down an old school friend. He knocked on the door of the immediate neighbor of where his school friend once lived, only to be confronted by a hostile resident who told him he had no idea who lived next door. My friend asked how long the neighbor had lived there, to which the neighbor replied "eighteen years"! It was incomprehensible to us that someone could live next door to another for eighteen years and not even know their neighbor's name.

The loss of community has resulted in the loss of something precious, core, and instrumental to our sense of belonging, fulfillment, and happiness. Something vital to our overall sense of well-being has been lost and we need to reclaim it. Any challenge carries with it a seed of opportunity. It is possible to co-create sustainable lifestyles within a city or town if there is a network of like minds. It then becomes possible to trade on an exchange basis and co-create the conditions required for sustainable living. Perhaps we would do well to gather in places more in tune with nature, rather than at the local pub? Not that there is anything wrong with the local pub, itself a hub of the local community. A far more satisfying pint of beer or glass of wine are to be had following an afternoon exchanging skills that help to support each other. The good feelings of a community united in action strengthen the bonds between its members. Taking care of the community's elders, by cooking meals that they can stock in their freezers, doing odd jobs around their homes, or taking them somewhere by car will help cultivate a strong sense of community.

We could gather together in neighborhoods to sow seeds; then, as the season turns, we could together reap the harvest in community spirit. Such a city or town lifestyle would also put us back in touch with the seasons, the phases of the moon, the elements, and nature.

A SPIRITUAL FAMILY HOME

Some of you may feel that creating a beautiful and uplifting home, one that feels calm and peaceful, is impossible if you have children or teenagers. Yet it *is* possible, if we are willing to model a new set of values to our youngsters.

In the West, children are raised very differently from those in Eastern countries who are taught from birth to respect their elders, the home, and the environment. In Tibet, every house has a room dedicated to spirituality with an altar and many spiritual offerings. Tibetan parents will take infants into this sacred space and from a tender age these children are taught how to behave in such a space. By the time they are toddlers they are sitting quietly and respectfully with their parents in these sacred rooms in meditation and prayer. They are not forced to do so but because of the parenting ways of Tibetans, who treat children with gentleness and respect, they develop a deep trust and respect for their elders and therefore naturally long to be in their company.

In Tibetan, Indian, Thai, Japanese, Chinese, Malaysian, and many other Eastern country homes, the honoring of spiritual energies is not confined to just one room. The whole house will reflect reverence through the use of incense and burning oils and the display of beautiful flowers, spiritual mantras, and imagery. These countries may be poorer than those in the West, but their spiritual values enrich them in a way that we rarely experience in our part of the world, despite all of our material possessions. We do not have to be materially rich to create peace and beauty within our homes, only spiritually wealthy. When we feel peace and beauty within ourselves we manifest the same in our lives.

Rather than just accepting that children and teenagers are unruly or disrespectful because "that is the nature of being young" (which it is not), we need to recognize that the values we instill in our young in the West are desperately in need of changing. We need to acknowledge that the Western culture is out of balance, as are we as adults, which is reflected in our parenting approach, our behavior, and our homes. This in turn influences our teenagers, children, and toddlers who then follow our examples as role models. This is a sign of the times. These are changing, however, and we need to create new boundaries within our homes to guide our children, not by commanding, demanding, expecting, or shouting, which only serve to exacerbate rebellion, but instead by using love, kindness, gentleness, and respect. Then we begin to make it possible for our homes to reflect peace and tranquility as our youngsters gain a new found sense of self-worth and respect for the adults whom they emulate.

THE INNER TEMPLE

How can the body help you to raise your vibration? Your body is a sacred place, the temple of the soul. How you relate to your body, how you treat your body, and your attitude toward your physicality is important. Take a few minutes to learn more about your attitude by answering the following questions:

- Just how do you feel about your body?
- What do you think about your body?
- What does your body mean to you?
- Do you regard it as merely a machine that needs fuel to keep it going?
- Is it something you would rather not think about at all because of the discomfort you feel about it?

- Is your body something that you place heavy demands upon in terms of exercising or pushing it to its limits?
- Or do you think of your body as an unfortunate byproduct of being human and prefer to disassociate from it?
- Perhaps your body has been the cause of restriction for you in this life?
- Maybe you have been plagued by illness or accidents?
- Do you feel ashamed of your body and wish you had another one instead?
- Or could it be that you are overly attached to your body and how it looks, and thus place too much emphasis on the attention it brings you?
- Do you loathe your body for the unwanted attention that it gets you?
- Or do you appreciate your body for the wondrous miracle that it is?

Which of these most accurately fit your experience? What we need to remind ourselves is that we *have* a body but we *are not* our body. In having a body, let us love, appreciate, and care for it, for it is doing its best to support us while we resolve karma, manage the ascension process, and evolve toward enjoying the gift of being alive in a body.

Many of the issues we have at a physical level, in terms of how we feel about our bodies, have their roots in childhood and past lives. By working deeply with these issues we can begin to heal the origins of our discomforts. The *feelings* and *thoughts* we hold in relation to our bodies serve to either raise or lower our vibration. On a more physical level, our thoughts and feelings induce powerful chemical reactions or responses that either promote wellness or exacerbate illness. As Bruce Lipton tells us, "Good news makes you well, bad news makes you ill."

To help raise your vibration you can start by looking at and improving your diet. Get clean from the inside out. Detox and eat ORGANIC! Cut down on coffee and tea and try to drink at least two quarts of water a day. Eat plenty of green leafy vegetables as well as a varied selection of other vegetables and salads. Make the preparation of salads fun. Create red salads from red peppers, cranberries, radishes, and tomatoes, purple salads from red cabbage, beets, purple sprouting broccoli, and blueberries. Try green salads with salad leaves, avocado, green peppers, and celery. Exchange wheat products for wheat-free, rye, oat, or spelt options. Cut out red meat and instead eat responsibly sourced fish or organic, free-range chicken once or twice a week. Eat more pulses like lentils, chickpeas, butter beans, aduki beans, and kidney beans. You can make fabulous dishes with pulses! Replace sweets and chocolate with dried fruits like mangos, papaya, pineapple, and banana. If you eat chocolate, try to make it organic.

Whatever you put onto your skin is absorbed into the blood stream. Be mindful of the products you use. People wonder why there is such a proliferation of cancers and other debilitating and life-threatening illnesses in the modern world. Could this have anything to do with our choice of lifestyles, as many of us live in or near polluted areas and smother our bodies in chemicals, from perfumes and colognes to deodorants and shower gels? The use of chemical-laden products on our bodies, even the hair dyes we use, can be detrimental to our health. Choose healthy, organic, chemical-free options.

Exercise more but make it manageable. You do not need to go to the expense of joining a gym or a health club, nor do you need to go running or cycling, especially along a polluted road! Go for a walk or a swim. Get an exercise bike and put it near a window (or outside on a nice day) and cycle each day for a period of time. You can use two tins of soup (organic of course!) as arm weights. Buy a hoola hoop to tone your waist. If you are to able join a yoga, tai chi, or pilates class, do. If you do not have time to do so, there are plenty of DVDs to teach you in the comfort of your own home. Go out dancing, enroll in dance lessons, or put on your old favorites at home and dance! All of these will uplift you. If you are restricted with a disability you can still exercise, whether by listening to music and swaying to it in your bed or wheelchair, or gently lifting your limbs. "Finding" yourself in your favorite piece of music will transport you, uplift you, and flood your system with endorphins and serotonin as well as other biochemical responses, which will positively impact your health.

Nourish your body, mind, and soul. You may wish to join a meditation class or attend psychospiritual or health-related workshops, seminars, or perhaps healthy eating cooking courses. These are wonderful ways to meet like minds and establish life-long bonds of friendship.

There are certain people on the planet, many of whom are found in the healing arena, who can have an enormously positive impact on our well-being. They can also profoundly impact our consciousness and expand our perception simply by our being within the field of their lightbody. These remarkable world healers can be likened to "tuning forks" and are able to help us to fine tune ourselves. When we enter the energy field of such a person we experience an alteration in our thought and feeling patterns as our vibration begins to synchronize with the energetic field of such Earthly luminaries. When in the company of highly developed healers and spiritual teachers we may experience powerful responses, including weeping, exaltation, altered states of consciousness, psychic flashes, insights, visions, and an enhanced state of well-being.

CHAPTER TWELVE

The Lost Mode of Prayer

The secret of our lost mode of prayer is to shift our perspective of life by feeling that the miracle has already happened and our prayers have been answered. Now we have the opportunity to bring this wisdom into our lives as prayers of gratitude for what already exists, rather than asking for our prayers to be answered.

GREGG BRADEN, *SECRETS OF THE LOST MODE OF PRAYER: THE HIDDEN POWER OF BEAUTY, BLESSINGS, WISDOM, AND HURT*

Our spiritual heritage has become distorted beyond recognition by a religion that has become institutionalized. One of the most emotive and sacred aspects of our spiritual heritage is the mode of *prayer*. Many religions have reduced the act of praying to one of "bargaining," "pleading," and "begging." In such a context the success of this profoundly humble act and the supplicant's worth is measured only by whether or not the prayer is answered. The understanding of prayer has been distorted and we have a disempowered connection with God/Source as a result. We approach prayer as meek or needy and see the God of religion as the all-powerful force that decides if we are worthy enough to have our prayer answered.

Many of us experience prayer as something we do when we are in great need, such as when a loved one is sick or dying or when we wish to improve our lives or the lives of those around us. Our learned rituals for prayer require us to be on our knees or to sit with hands clasped together fervently, asking for what we need in the hope that it just might be given to us. What we have forgotten is that prayer is as natural to the human soul as breathing, and that by praying we can reconnect to God, the Source that lies within us. Because of the religious conditioning of two thousand years, we fail to realize that through the act of calling in the angels, our spiritual helpers, and the higher dimensions, we enhance our connection to our own God Self, so can also answer our own prayers.

What has been lost today is our sixth sense of gnosis, that inborn gift of *inner knowing* and the true expression of wisdom. Gnosis reveals that a prayer is a *feeling*. Its effectiveness has nothing to do with our thoughts or emotions and everything to do with feeling. To pray in the truest sense is to *feel the feeling* of the very thing it is we are praying for. We *feel the feeling* as if it has already happened.

In contrast, if you are unwell and are praying for recovery, you may say, "Dear God, please help me to become well again." This communicates to your higher Self (your God Self to whom you are praying, for we are all God), your DNA, your luminous energy field, and the environment that you are unwell, which further compounds this statement as a belief system and an experience. You are telling yourself you would like to become well again but you are placing that possibility outside of yourself, by requesting "outside" assistance from a higher Source. What needs to be understood is that this higher Source is not separate from you in anyway; it is both within and without. This higher Source is you and you are it. By praying to be well and happy, for inner peace and abundance, you are acknowledging that this state does not yet exist and therefore the environment, which is simply a mirror, will reflect this back to you. As you continue to pray for what you need, you will reinforce your neediness.

PRAYERS, WISHES, AND MIRACLES—
THE ALCHEMICAL ART OF PLAYING

Prayers have been confused with wishes and wishes have been confused with miracles. But each of these is an entirely different form of manifestation. The prayers of religious belief have reduced us to a market stall mentality, where we barter for our needs. We bargain with a higher power saying, for example, "If you make this possible I'll never swear again," and so on. By using prayer as "wish-making," we find that we pray even harder for our wishes to come true. Or we treat prayers as miracles—they are not. *We* are the miracle and when we realize the truth of this, miracles will occur naturally in our lives, as they are meant to. Recognizing that we are a living miracle can be as simple as being aware of our capacity to breathe, think, talk, walk, taste, see, hear, feel, heal. All of these are natural occurrences. All of these are miracles.

Modern day praying is often accompanied by a sense of guilt for the lack of spiritual or religious connection present in our lives in general. Because the art of praying, wishing, and miracles has been so distorted, we have lost the understanding that they are natural phenomena.

Prayers, wishes, and miracles are three very different spiritual gifts that humans have been playing with (*playing* refers to the joy, delight, fun, and pleasure that these gifts bestow on us) for thousands of years. The origins of prayer date further back in time than Jesus, to advanced civilizations such as Atlantis, which disappeared about 13,000 years ago. These highly evolved cultures knew how to *play* with the art of prayer, wishes, and miracles. The ancients may not have referred to this art as praying or prayer, but the practice was the same, *to feel the feeling* of what they were seeking to manifest. Making wishes, an ancient alchemical practice associated with mystery and magic, is an art that has also been lost to us.

Prayers, wishes, and miracles are alchemical acts and the time has now come to reclaim these lost arts and learn to *play* with mystery and magic to create beauty, abundance, joy, and wonder. All three result in *manifestation.* Much is now written about manifestation and the many techniques designed to help us achieve this, most of which engage the mind. The art of manifestation was originally about engaging the *feelings.* I sense that we are beginning to remember what we once knew about alchemy and that the recent popularity with manifestation techniques and principles will lead us back to its purer origins. By engaging the heart and our feelings from a place of openness, excitement, wonder, joy, and gnosis, what we feel in that moment will become real.

Religion invites "Let us pray." I suggest, "Let us play." You may like to try a little exercise. With eyes open or closed, *feel what it feels like to be well.* By doing this you are sending a message to yourself and the surrounding quantum field (divine matrix) and flooding your entire system with feelings of radiance, wellness, and wholeness. This prayer instructs your DNA to respond to the information, which is then relayed to the divine matrix. *Feeling* is the union between *thought and emotion* and is expressed through the heart, which is the source of *the felt sense. Feeling the feeling* of wellness invites your luminous energy field and the quantum field to mirror this back to you. Wellness will lead to wellness. However, if we pray to be well we may find ourselves coming down with a cold the next day! The "news" you give yourself has the power to make you well or ill, joyful or woeful.

The ancient mode of prayer is ultimately a moment of pure self-empowerment. It is a moment when we speak our prayers as if they are a *reality,* already alive. The art of prayer is to *feel the feeling as if the prayer has already been answered.* Indigenous peoples *feel the feeling* of gratitude at the beginning of each day, anticipating what wonderful things are going to happen. This allows the luminous energy body and the quantum field to respond accordingly. It is a communion—a "common union" between Source intelligence within us and God/Source intelligence. Praying (feeling) influences the luminous energy field and the quantum field, which in turn reflect back to us what we are *feeling,* at a personal and impersonal level.

Part of true prayer is being aware of the source of our prayer. Is it from the depth of our hearts, our souls, or is it from a place of fear and need? Remember, the field will respond to what we project into it. The "Medicineless" hospital in China filmed a true prayer session (see Gregg Braden's *The Science of Miracles* DVD). Three hospital assistants surrounded a "patient" who had an inoperable bladder tumor, while another held a scanning device recording the tumor on a screen monitor. Alongside the "live" recording of the tumor in one half of the screen was a still image of the tumor taken before treatment commenced. Simultaneously, the assistants and the patient began to *feel the feeling* of the patient as healthy. They chanted statements that reinforced the patient's wellness and in less than three minutes the tumor had gone. This was captured live on camera.

THE LOST MODE OF PRAYER
AS AN ANTIDOTE TO TRAUMA AND CRIME

In *The Science of Miracles,* Gregg Braden reveals how a group of people trained in the lost mode of prayer were strategically positioned in twenty-four cities across the U.S. in 1972. They all focused their intent on *feeling the feeling* of peace at the same time. Statistically, measurable reductions in crime, traffic accidents, and emergency room (ER) admissions were recorded in all twenty-four cities during that window of prayer. When the prayer ended the statistics reverted back to normal. This experiment was conducted several times to measure the findings and each result was the same—a dramatic decrease in activities involving trauma and crime.

Princeton University in the U.S. conducted a research program titled "The Global Consciousness Project," which proved that our feelings affect the quantum field around us. Braden goes on to share how the same principles were applied during the Israeli-Lebanese war in the mid 1980s. This experiment, documented in the *Journal of Conflict Resolution* in 1988, was called, "The International Peace Project of the

Middle East." People were placed in war-torn areas to *feel the feeling of peace*. During the window of prayer, terrorist activity dropped to zero. Experiments took place on different days, weekends, or months at varying times and it was found that when people prayed in unison, *feeling the feeling of peace,* the results were always the same. Distance is not a factor, as experiments conducted over the Internet with thousands of people across the world have proved. Statisticians have determined that the exact amount of people required to *feel the feeling* in order to trigger this kind of effect is the square root of one percent of a given target population.

There are approximately six billion people on the planet and the amount needed to *feel the feeling of peace,* in unison, to effect a significant change is just 8,000. However, these prayers must come from the depths of the heart and soul. They must be what I term as a "whole body" prayer, whereby we feel the energy of love and conviction flowing from our cells, our organs, our skin, and into the quantum field. By permeating the quantum field we can bring a sense of peace back into the world. Belief is a powerhouse of potential. Jesus told us: "You can renew your life with your beliefs," and two thousand years later, quantum physics and science are now telling us the same thing.

Six billion people are communicating with the quantum field *all of the time.* This field is a reflection of the collective consciousness and is mirrored back to us. We need only look at the world to understand the emotional, mental, and psychological state of the billions that inhabit it. We must recognize that whatever we feel, whenever we feel it, and wherever we feel it, that feeling will exist everywhere. We do not need to send our prayers outward; we simply *feel the feeling* of what we choose for ourselves, each other, and the world, as if it already is, and it will instantly register everywhere.

These quantifiable facts illustrate how we can heal ourselves and each other. We are only just beginning to scratch the surface of what is possible. It is detrimental to think we are sick, fearful, or sad. It is important that we see everyone and the Earth herself as well, loved, happy, and fulfilled. As human beings, our nature is one that thrives on support and connection with others. A gathering of two or three or more can be a potent way to affect the change we wish to see.

THE ORIGINAL PRAYER

A feeling is a prayer. It is the original prayer. A feeling is prayer in its purest, most potent form. Whether we are in love, peace, joy, fear, sadness, or anger, we are praying all of the time, for our feelings are prayers. Human beings are *feeling* beings and because of that, life is a living prayer. As long as we can hold peace, love, and joy in our hearts, our lives on Earth will reflect that living prayer.

All that we yearn for, the beauty, joy, love, fulfillment, unity, harmony, and peace, is only a *prayer* away. Imagine what life on Earth would be like if six billion people were all having the same feelings of love and beauty at the same time? It can start with just one person and spread throughout the world. Remember, it takes only 8,000 of the world's population to effect a change, albeit temporary. Imagine the potential for permanent global transformation, if six billion people were radiating love all the time.

Transform *your* feelings and *you* transform the world.

CHAPTER THIRTEEN

The Grail in the Heart

Every individual who becomes a clear and undistorted channel
for eternal love into these times offsets a thousand who remain
locked in the dissolving values of the old.

KEN CAREY, *STARSEED: THE THIRD MILLENNIUM*

At the heart of any great adventure lies the quest, the quest for something lost. At the center of the human heart is the grail, the golden sacred receptacle that contains the elixir of life. This grail overflows with a magical and alchemical energy that flows like a river pouring light into our entire energetic system, regenerating and empowering us, connecting us to our purpose, at both a personal and planetary level. Just as blood is pumped around the body by the physical heart, so too is this light and energy distributed around the physical system, making us feel well, vibrant, and radiant. The experience of this light and energy translates into the physical as a *feel good factor*. This sacred elixir causes the energetic and physical system to vibrate at a higher level and radiate a tangible light. To fully experience this we need to reconnect to our core Self, the *true* expression of who we really are. This authentic Self *is* the grail; our quest is to rediscover it and, by doing so, embody the higher purpose of our soul.

The place where we begin our search is in the very place we feel it to be missing, in our hearts. The true colors of the heart at an energetic level are intensely rich, deep, soft, and vibrant. These energetic tones of the heart range from rosy pinks, rich reds, exquisitely gentle greens, deep and intense purples, to pure shades of violet, white, and gold. However, when we are unhappy, unfulfilled, sad, or in pain, the heart will appear flecked or saturated with grey, brown, and black tones. The heart can also contain a combination of different shades, each expressing an aspect of our inner psychospiritual state.

☽ Finding the Grail

You might like to try this little exercise. This is an exercise for the soul (the imagination in action), so allow your *senses* to inform you. You do not need to understand it at a cognitive level. Trust what you are *sensing*. Trust the imagery that arises, no matter how unrelated or abstract it might seem.

1. Go into your imagination for a moment, perhaps close your eyes, and invite an image that represents the color of your heart. Trust the first image that appears.

2. What do you see? How many shades are in your heart? What color or colors do you see? What does your heart look like? Does your energetic heart appear to you as an image of something else? What is your heart showing you? What does your heart need? What does your heart know? If your heart had a voice, what would it say? Can you see the grail in your heart and, if so, describe what you see? If not, what is there? Where is the grail? Allow your imagination to show you what is there.

3. Now open your eyes and sit for a few moments, reflecting on what you have just seen. You may want to write down or sketch the hidden messages your heart has revealed.

For those who did not see or sense anything, could it be that you are so used to *thinking* that you have forgotten how to *sense?* You may need to try this exercise as you are going to sleep or just as you are waking, when your brainwaves are in what is known as *theta,* the hypnogogic/hypnotic state, which is the realm of the creative imagination. If this does not work for you, it may be valuable to join a creative expression group, an art class, or visit a hypnotherapist who works with guided visualization. It does not take long at all for the right brain to become active and, once it does, it will enhance your life and dramatically alter your perception of yourself, other people, and the world around you.

YOUR SPECIAL GIFT

As we move closer to the Shift of Ages it cannot be overemphasized that we have only a small window of time to bring about significant changes within ourselves and the world, if we are to experience true peace at an inner and outer level. Each one of us holds a position of *response-ability* as we move closer to December 21, 2012. Each one of us is a steward for this planet, charged with the responsibility to maintain her in a state of wellness and balance. It is time for those of us who are willing to step forward to roll up our sleeves, take a deep breath, and help to facilitate the most important crossing of a threshold for humanity in recorded history. We are on the point of entering unity consciousness, an occurrence that can and will positively transform the world.

You may already have an awareness of the gift you bring to the world. If not, this will reveal itself in your daydreams, night journeys, and aspirations and through those who inspire you. We currently operate at two levels: the *personality* level (the conditioned ego self) and the level of the higher Self. Many live predominantly at a personality (ego) level, while others are more connected with their higher, more altruistic nature (higher Self). Then there are those who are connected with both, some of whom are caught up at a personality level in fear, "shoulds," and "oughts," resulting in dysfunctional, inauthentic lives. Such people trade their true hopes and dreams for conformity. How many of us have shared our aspirations with our families and peers, only to be told to "stop dreaming" or that we are "getting above ourselves"?

What do you really wish to do with your life? What dreams have you shelved for the sake of "fitting in" with the expectations of others? What did you give up or sacrifice? Maybe the time wasn't right then, but it is now. Allow yourself to pause and think for a moment. What most inspires you? What most excites you? What would make your heart sing? What would you really like to be doing with your life, given the opportunity? Remember that opportunities are self-created. How much are you compromising your hopes, dreams, and aspirations?

You may have a job in an office and yet long to assist people to swim with dolphins. You may work in a supermarket or bank and harbor visions of working in Africa, caring for orphaned elephant calves. Perhaps you are unemployed and dream of being out in the world doing what you most love to do? For example, you may be the one family and friends turn to with their problems. If so, why not train in something that comes naturally to you as a counselor? In some places government support for education or setting up a new business is available. You may be raising a young family; you can still create or get involved with something that inspires you.

If you are housebound, unwell, disabled, or live in an institution and find yourself wondering how you can make a difference and contribute to the Clarion Call from the higher realms, try not to dismiss yourself as being incapable of making an important contribution because of any physical challenges or restrictions. You have a beautiful creative mind, which can express itself through writing, study, design, or other creative activities. If you have a telephone you can work as a telephone counselor. If you have access to a computer and telephone this allows you to be anywhere in the world at the click of a button, to exchange information and share ideas, set up websites, blogs, set up a recording studio, or film YouTube interviews via your laptop. You could even write a book about your life that may serve to inspire many others.

You can be a positive influence without physically having to be anywhere other than the place you consider home. Instead, you can unite with others energetically, via the worldwide web and through the mind. You can make a difference, no matter how great or small. Your contribution could be the critical *one* that takes us over that threshold into a golden millennium. Regardless of your circumstances, your life has an impact. By acting with unconditional loving-kindness and nonjudgmental acceptance of all whom you encounter, you can substantially contribute to the great changes ahead. The difference a kind voice and a warm and loving smile can make is immeasurable.

If you feel that fear or lack of self-worth is holding you back or if there is a possibility that you unconsciously sabotage your altruistic intentions, then the time has come for you to make the commitment to change your life. *Let your courage be stronger than your fear.* You alone can do this. Are you willing to transcend your conditioned personality and follow the vision of your soul? You may need to reach out for support, and the resource directory at the back of the book will help you to find just what you need. There are many evolved teachers, guides, books, DVDs and audio CDs, as well as the Internet, which will inspire you to transform your self-perception and how you experience the world.

You are being asked not to underestimate the urgency of this Clarion Call or how much each one of you is needed. It is important to recognize that we are now working against a clock. As a global community we simply do not have time to procrastinate if we want to live in a peace-loving world. Humanity needs to *wake up* at this critical juncture in history. It is imperative that we remain mindful of our thoughts, words, and actions and how these impact others. If we are fundamentalist, dictatorial, bullying, or coercive we are not aligning with the light. We are requested by the heavenly realms to conduct ourselves with integrity and an open heart.

Because of the single-minded focus and dedication required by those of us who are engaged in the transformation of human consciousness during these next few years, we are not expected to balance our time between personal healing and our worldly mission. Commitment to this cause must take precedence in our lives these next two years if humanity is to successfully cross into a new world on the winter solstice of 2012. That is why the Divine Dispensation from the Luminous Ones placed at the beginning of this book was channeled through me during the writing of this book. It is our *response-ability* to conduct ourselves in an *impeccable* manner and lead by example. It is our task to be role models for *unconditional positive regard* and *nonjudgment* and *to express loving-kindness* to all and especially to those who may turn to us for guidance.

PERSONAL INQUIRY

As we draw closer to the winter solstice of 2012, we need to align our personality with our soul and embrace ourselves and our lives from this exalted place. Here are some questions you might like to reflect upon. Trust the first feeling/image/sound that arises as you ask yourself each question. Take time to *feel* your response. Pause after each question to give yourself time for reflection, feeling, and intuition. Write or sketch your responses to help ground your insights.

- Are you willing to put aside your personality/ego and attachment to old dysfunctional patterns and commit yourself fully to the 2012 cause?
- Do you feel that it is possible for you move out of your own way? If not, what do you need in order to be able to do so?
- Are you willing to make a pact between your personality/ego, your higher Self, and your spirit guides and teachers to devote the remaining years until 2012 to serve the highest good?
- Are you willing to immediately disengage from self-limiting beliefs, patterns, and mindsets, as well as those people and situations around you that limit the true expression of your soul during these next few years?

If, in responding to the above inquiries, you are aware of any resistance or hesitation, be curious about why that is. If, however, you have answered "Yes" to all of these questions, roll up your sleeves, as now is the moment to begin the spiritual, humanitarian, ecological, and environmental task ahead.

Summary

There are many accounts and explanations of what 2012 represents. By adding my own contribution to these, I hope to help bring some clarity and offer a grounded and accurate overview of all that has been written about the 2012 phenomena.

There are some who are afraid that the world will end in the winter of 2012. Others feel we are going to disappear in a puff of heavenly smoke and leave the Earth altogether. Then there are those who believe that we are to be rescued or attacked by extraterrestrials, while still more believe we will no longer need our physical bodies in the way we do now and therefore will have no need of a material way of living. It is not surprising that there is so much confusion around the date of 2012!

My intention has been to offer you an accurate account of what is unfolding leading to December 21, 2012, to help you become better informed, as well as to offer sound advice and guidance on how you can benefit at a psychospiritual level by participating with the auspicious energies that are now available to help each of us with our personal process of transformation.

This book offers insights into why these indeed are momentous times. It has introduced you to the concept of the consciousness-transforming wisdom that we have inherited from highly evolved teachers who lived before, as well as what we are receiving in the present day from those who live among us and those who are yet to come.

There are no coincidences. In reading this book you have responded to a call from your higher Self, from the higher realms, and from the Luminous Ones, who have communicated with you through its words and guidance. *2012: A Clarion Call* seeks to encourage you not to stand on the sidelines as a mere witness, watching history in the making, but instead calls for your true Self to become a participant in and contributor to the unique events that are unfolding.

This book is a Clarion Call to remind you of who you truly are and how important your soul contribution is in these critical times. As the Hopis say: "We are the ones we have been waiting for." The next few years represent the greatest call to humanity in the history of the Earth. This is a *global* Clarion Call and it is hoped that this book might just encourage you to take positive, peaceful action and become a beacon of light for the world. Your love and wisdom are needed on the frontline of the 2012 threshold, a unifying moment, when the world needs the greatest light to transcend the dark path we are currently trading.

This is your chance to *shine*, to know what it feels like to live with a purpose that extends beyond your personal world and connects you with all of humanity, the Earth, and the universe. This is the chance of a lifetime to truly know how it feels to be fulfilling your destiny. These next few years that lead to the winter solstice of 2012 present you with a golden opportunity to be honored by Great Spirit, no matter who you are or what you have done in this life or past lives, for daring to have the courage to stand up and be counted upon.

This is an invitation for ALL to cooperate and unite as one mind, one heart, one people, to create a better world and future. Responding to this call can transform your life into the life of your dreams. Being able to hold your head high with the knowledge that you have made a difference, no matter how small, will accelerate the clearing and dissolving of karma and redirect you to a life that is influenced and shaped by the good you have done.

This Clarion Call points toward infinite possibilities and holds the potential to catalyze a radical change in your consciousness, one that can realign you with your soul's higher purpose. You are being encouraged to *remember* and, by doing so, unite with the tens of thousands of other global torchbearers who are also *remembering* what they have chosen to contribute toward the greatest chance we have for world peace in modern history. Your support is urgently needed to guide and influence those on the old path across the pivotal 2012 threshold. Your individual role is critical to ensure that humanity fulfills profound ancient prophecies. The great wise ones who have brought this book into being implore you to open your heart and hold out your hand to all those who need assistance in making this momentous transition.

The ultimate purpose of this book has been to encourage and guide you to fully awaken, to realize the true and higher purpose of your soul, to offer you ways to raise your consciousness and vibration. These are all key components of insuring the overall planetary vibration is raised sufficiently to allow us to successfully cross the 2012 threshold into a prophesied Golden Age, which promises "a thousand years of peace."

I offer it to you in love, truth, and peace.

May you join me in making the following pledge, which was channeled through me during the writing of this book:

Dedication Pledge

On this day, I pledge myself in service to the highest good of humanity and the Earth.

With my life, my heart and soul, I shall do my best to ensure that the gift of my presence here on Earth in these times is dedicated to supporting the great transition of 2012.

May the gift of my life prove to be an asset for my earthly brothers and sisters, the four legged, two legged, finned, furred, winged ones, and insects,

and for all animate and inanimate energy forms here on the Earth.

May it ever be so.

Let Your Courage Be Stronger Than Your Fear

Miracle and the Birth of This Book

We Lakota people have a prophecy about the white buffalo calf: When a white female buffalo calf is born and turns color from white to yellow, from black to red and then to white again, there will come a time of great peace, harmony, and balance among mankind.

TRADITIONAL LAKOTA QUOTE

WHO IS MIRACLE?

Miracle is the sacred white buffalo born August 20, 1994, on the family farm of Valerie and David Heider in Janesville, Wisconsin, USA, land that was historically the home of ancient Native Americans. She was the first all-white, non-albino, female buffalo to be born since 1933, when a white buffalo male calf was born. According to statistics from the National Buffalo Association, the chances of the birth of a white, non-albino, female buffalo is somewhere in the region of one in six billion. Most importantly, Miracle's birth fulfilled a two-thousand-year-old prophecy of the Lakota, Dakota, and Nakota Plains Indians known collectively as the Sioux.

More than two thousand years ago a Great Being known as "White Buffalo Calf Woman" appeared to the Lakota people. Before taking human form she appeared to the plains Indians of that time in the shape of a white buffalo. White Buffalo Calf Woman gave the Lakota ancestors a sacred pipe and sacred ceremonies and made them guardians of the Black Hills. She introduced them to a new way of living, giving them sacred laws and a spiritual creed by which they still live to this day. Before departing she prophesied that one day she would return to purify the world, bringing back spiritual balance and harmony to all of humanity.

During her visit she told the Native Americans that the birth of a white female buffalo calf would be a sign that her return was imminent. She foretold that the sacred white female buffalo calf would change color four times. When she left, she transformed into a white buffalo calf and rolled over four times. The first time, she turned into a yellow buffalo, the second time into a black one, the third time she turned red, and finally she turned back into a white female buffalo calf. The sacred pipe given by White Buffalo Calf Woman is still kept in South Dakota by Chief Arvol Lookinghorse, the nineteenth-generation Keeper of the Sacred White Buffalo Calf Pipe Bundle.

Miracle also held special significance for many other Native American nations as well as other indigenous cultures across the globe. But it is specifically the Lakota prophecies that she fulfills. She is female and the bull that sired her died shortly following her birth, just as the prophecy foretold. The prophecy stated that "the white buffalo calf would change color four times." Miracle turned from white to yellow, from yellow to black, and from black to red. This is not usual for white buffalo calves. All other white buffalo calves have remained white or whitish. As Miracle grew into an adult she developed a reddish brown coat typical of a buffalo.

A Lakota Sioux medicine man stated shortly following Miracle's birth that "the arrival of this white, female buffalo calf is like the second coming of Christ. It will bring about purity of mind, body, and spirit and unify all nations, black, red, yellow, and white." The Lakota, Dakota, and Nakota nations were considered Miracle's primary spiritual guardians throughout her lifetime since she played a pivotal role in the fulfillment of their most revered prophecies. As the prophecy foretold, after turning the four colors, she would then blend with the herd until humankind came together, at which point she would once again turn white.

Unexpectedly, aged just ten, Miracle died of natural causes on September 19, 2004. This was unusual as buffalos can live for thirty years. However, Miracle did everything that the prophecy said she would do, except turn white for a second time. No one will ever know if she would have gone back to her original color. However, she had begun to lighten again but her death interrupted any further changes.

It has been estimated that over one million people visited the little farm in Wisconsin where she was born and lived and over half a million have visited her website. Imagine how many more have learned about her through those who know of her. Miracle's life touched millions of people, each one absorbing the message of forthcoming peace and harmony for humanity.

STEPPING INTO THE UNKNOWN

After Miracle appeared to me in April 2009, and I was encouraged by her presence and that of the Luminous Ones to write this book, I experienced a specific process that showed me what others may encounter were they to choose to align with their higher purpose. What was brought to my attention, most forcibly, was the polarity between fear and courage, ignorance and wisdom, personality and soul. I immediately became aware of these within myself, understanding how as the inner light burns brighter, so too will the shadow edges become exposed in order to be acknowledged and healed. This intense spotlight revealed personality-level blocks and issues I had been convinced were no longer a part of my experience, specifically those of fear and self-doubt.

As I confronted residual shadow issues, an inner dialogue began. I had never written a book, I reminded myself. Neither had I any formal training that would qualify me to do so. In fact, those who know me would vouch for the fact that one of my personal edges centers around a marked lack of understanding of academic or intellectual material. Having once had a photographic memory, I now experience a severely impaired memory that renders me virtually speechless in any group setting or debate, as I cannot hold on to concepts for any more than a few fleeting seconds. I am able, however, to fully absorb information at a felt level, even though I am unable to comprehend it at a mental level. Friends, many of whom are intellectually gifted, can repeat themselves ad infinitum and in an instant I will forget everything they have told me. Yet the feeling resonates strongly within me and informs me in an entirely different way. What I do have is a natural and highly developed ability to intuit, sense, and feel, and these gifts entirely influence the choices I make in my life.

What I have come to realize is that I assimilate information in quite a different way than most people and that my mind *is* highly developed. Several years ago, I was wired up to a machine that measures brain activity. The doctor who conducted the test is a specialist in brain research. She informed me that she had never seen the area of the brain that represents "spiritual" activity be so developed and active. I am not saying that such a test measures spiritual development: I am merely pointing out the fact that my brain operates in quite an abstract way, seeming to struggle with concrete information, yet excelling in abstract (gnosis). Everything I experience filters through my senses, through what I describe as my "receptors," which have become highly developed as a result of the way I naturally process the world I live in.

I have struggled most of my life with our culture's current "measuring" system that determines intelligence. I understand now that my intelligence operates differently and that, from a soul perspective, there is a reason that I chose for this to be so. The fact that I am unable to retain information proves an asset for me as a sensitive and a channel: I can be quite sure that there is no way the information I receive is stored in my conscious memory. Perhaps this is why this book has come through me. Being invited by Miracle and the Luminous Ones to embark upon this spiritual work shone a light on how my deeper fears and self-doubts had still not been fully healed. Uncomfortable emotions and thoughts would arise each time I seriously considered proceeding with what I had been invited to do. Had I listened to my rational mind and anxieties you would not be reading these words today.

Fully aligning with the higher purpose of the soul makes it possible to heal core wounds naturally, as we are able to access the core blockages while connecting with the magnificence of who we really are. Truly aligning with soul purpose calls forth the higher Self, which gives our lives deep meaning. However, for this to occur the personality (ego/historical wounds) needs to be healed and integrated. The energy of the higher Self carries an extraordinary purifying quality, which acts like a powerful beam of ultraviolet light, dissolving trauma imprints in the aura and thus bringing healing to our physical, emotional, mental, psychological, and energetic bodies.

The inner process that responding to the Clarion Call catalyzed showed me how to "get out of my own way," how to trust, surrender, and have courage and faith. It also encouraged me to embrace my deep understanding of gnosis. I was invited to truly stand in the center of my being and trust in gnosis, a knowing that is the result of the development of the soul, not the brain. And so it was: the teachings continued as I was pushed to the edge of my limits and into the realms of possibility. To be able to respond to the call from my higher Self, from Miracle and from the Luminous Ones, meant that it was necessary for me to live the message of the book. This has led me into a life of choices now rooted in trust, surrender, and gnosis.

A definite process was required of me to reach this place; owing to my wholehearted willingness to *trust* and *surrender,* the process proved to be a swift and painless one. There appeared to be an air of serendipity present and the universe seemed determined to give me the signs I needed to proceed with confidence. During one moment of wavering when I was in doubt about how to proceed, I received a telephone call, out of the blue, from Professor Stephen Brown from Exeter University in England, who had read an article that I had written (my first). He had felt compelled to contact me to ask if I had ever considered writing a book. My response was to explain that I had been thinking of doing so yet felt intellectually ill-equipped. Professor Brown completely disagreed with me, making a point of expressing how he experienced my writing as "unique" and how he felt I had something of great importance to convey through my writing. This phone call proved to be a turning point, as I began to accept that perhaps I *could* write a book.

Even though I understood that much of the information of the book would be guided, written through me by the Luminous Ones, still my anxieties persisted: "What if no one wants to publish it?" "What if no one wants to read it?" "What if it is successful and I have to be interviewed?" What if I set up workshops and sit there not knowing what to say because of my inability to memorize information and retain it?" "What if?" "What if?" "What if?"

At the same time that I was experiencing all these fears, the title *2012: A Clarion Call* blazed into my consciousness. I was shown the cover of the book, the CDs, workshop schedules, and all related material. I was shown that the time had come for sacred ancient prophecies to be understood and known by people across the world and how Miracle's influence would stand as testament to the 2012 prophecy coming to pass. I was shown the book and CDs being published and the workshops unfolding into great gatherings of people. I was even shown future interviews running smoothly!

Each time I went into utter fear about my financial situation, I was gently reassured by warm and loving Spirit energy that all would be well. I quickly understood that in order to write the book I would need to give up working with clients who were my sole source of income, as the book, audio scripts, and workshops would need to be written quickly, owing to the urgency of their content and the limited time frame available for a message that completes its purpose on the winter solstice of 2012. I had weeks to accomplish what would ordinarily take months or even years and had never attempted anything like it before. I remembered Donna White predicting that I would "channel six years of information in approximately six weeks." As it turned out, the book, the CD scripts, and workshop were written within six weeks.

Financially I had lived my life on the edge for many years, barely making ends meet. I had not had a holiday for over ten years, not even a weekend away, as funds were so low. I had financial commitments that relied upon client income and I knew I could not write a book and nine CD scripts and write and organize a workshop in a matter of weeks, while continuing to work at the same time,. The presence of the Luminous Ones became intense as I struggled with the challenge of how to make this possible. In the middle of April 2009 the Luminous Ones told me I needed to secure £6,000 to free my time to enable me to write *2012: A Clarion Call* and all that this would entail. I was assured that this sum would be made available by the end of that same month and would cover my financial needs for the period of time that I was writing and organizing all the material. I stifled a laugh wondering how on Earth I, with my financial history, was going to secure £6,000 in less than two weeks.

I was not aware of anyone who was able to loan me such an amount. I resisted trying to secure the funds via a loan and, once again, fear and doubt took over. What was exacerbating the situation was that my steady, albeit small, income had literally deteriorated overnight due to regular and new clients unexpectedly canceling sessions. I noted the perplexing absence of further appointments being booked.

I considered approaching my bank but decided against it, doubting they would even look at my application owing to my poor credit rating. I decided that the manifestation of £6,000 would be a sign that this Clarion Call experience was indeed real. If the money did not manifest, then I would sit and wonder for months to come just what this had all been about and attempt to work out what had happened regarding the sudden loss of my clients. I expressed to the Luminous Ones that, if the money manifested, I would surrender entirely to the task in hand, and if not, I would give up the whole idea as an experience where my psychic guidance had gone seriously wrong!

The days passed by with no sign of the necessary funds and I continued to experience fear and doubt. What is more, I began to feel physically nauseous each time I anticipated working with a client. The nausea became so extreme that I had no choice but to listen to its message, as it rendered me incapable of managing a client session save for the two who were still with me. I had no doubt that it was working with clients that triggered the intense nausea, as otherwise I felt fine.

My quest to secure these funds continued and I approached a few people privately without success and was left with no choice other than to contact the bank, as I now had virtually no income. With fear in one hand and courage in the other, I contacted the bank and was flatly turned down. What was happening? What was I to do? What had all this been about? How did I go from working with fourteen clients a week to two, overnight, who also informed me during that period that they would both complete their work with me a few weeks later! This was unprecedented, unexpected, and unplanned for.

The following day, after the failed bank request, I was sitting bewildered, with only two remaining clients, a mountain of bills, existing bank loan repayments, rent to pay, and a house move to pay for, attempting to make sense of what was happening, when the phone rang. It was the bank. They told me how they had found a small "loophole," which made it possible to loan me some money. I could not believe what I was hearing. "Yes," they were going to offer me a loan. "How much?" I tentatively asked, knowing that anything less than what I needed would not afford me the time to write the book, CDs, and the workshop. He replied, "£6,000." The money was in my bank within three days. The date was April 25, less than two weeks after the Luminous Ones assured me that £6,000 would be available to me by the end of April.

After Miracle first appeared she guided and influenced me in the writing of the book, along with the Luminous Ones. I continually felt that something profoundly special and magical was taking place. Miracle made it very clear what I was to do from our first encounter when I perceived her energy in the room with me and I trusted my gnosis and said "Yes!" This experience taught me that we should always trust our initial responses and work out the "how" later, or rather let the "how" work itself out. I "knew" I could not afford to immerse myself in such a huge undertaking, especially one with a time factor of only weeks. Yet this I achieved. For seven days a week, up to fifteen hours a day, I wrote, stopping only to eat, work with one or two clients, make the occasional mad dash to the local shop to buy essentials, or travel to view a house on the rare occasion one was available to rent.

It was necessary for me to experience this lightning speed process so that I could align with the higher purpose of my soul. In doing so, I was able to stand back and witness synchronicity after synchronicity unfold to bear testament to that. Because of Miracle and the presence of the Luminous Ones, my life has been forever changed. Through them I have experienced a deeper understanding of my own contribution to humanity. My fears and self-doubts have all but disappeared, the remedies being trust, surrender, faith, courage, and love. In a matter of moments, hours, days, I went from being unsure what I could offer to the world as my contribution in the approach to 2012, to fully embodying my purpose, a life-changing experience that words cannot express. My own response to the Clarion Call can serve to prove to you that in connecting to the higher purpose of your own soul, you can heal your deepest wounds and live your dreams. Your life can transform, if you allow yourself to be guided by higher Source intelligence and then trust.

Miracle's gift to us all is to help us connect as a collective consciousness to ancient soul memory and be reminded that we once lived in a Golden Age, right here on Earth, and that we have an opportunity do so again. The messages of the Luminous Ones serve to remind us all of the amazing potential that lies dormant or just beneath the surface within each one of us. I shall forever cherish the countless blessings that Miracle bestowed upon my life. I feel honored to have been approached by her great spirit, to help her fulfill part of her mission to reach many, many people and encourage them to unfold their magnificent wings and fly higher than they ever dreamed, as we collectively approach the great transition of 2012. I feel humbled to have been guided to this work by Miracle. The presence of this Sacred White Buffalo Spirit touches us all, as we prepare to support the coming changes and act as beacons of light as we help guide humanity in a new direction and into a new world paradigm.

May the Clarion Call encourage you to rise to the highest altitudes of your being, those mountainous ranges that are the dwelling place of your soul. May Miracle's message of hope for humanity and a coming era of peace and harmony encourage you to explore and be inspired by the ancient prophecies that tell of a new and Golden Era to reign on Earth from 2012.

My sense is that Miracle will be reborn after 2013, perhaps as another sacred white buffalo, perhaps as an aspect of Sacred White Buffalo Calf Woman, who prophesied her own return at this pivotal point in human history. My guidance shows me that Miracle left her body to serve the Earth from the higher dimensional realms. Miracle, along with the vast legions of multidimensional beings and ancient wise ones who guide this Earth, will be celebrating with us at the 2012 threshold, as we cross into a new era of world peace and unity. Let us honor and give thanks for Miracle's life and the hope her life has already given to millions of people. Miracle still walks among us, continuing to fulfill the Lakota prophecy.

Activating the Light-Body

Healing Methods and Practices

As the planet and humanity are subject to an increasing intensity of light, the result is an amplification of the dark. We are living in unprecedented times and each of us face immense challenges as the dark seeks to continue its control and hold over humanity. If we consciously choose to fully activate our individual Light-Body, then the highest-frequency light—the like of which has never been present on Earth—will spread across the planet at an extraordinary rate. This light will envelop the dark, transforming it into light. We have until December 21, 2012, to manifest this light, thus ensuring The Great Shift of Ages *the Ancient Wise Ones have prophesied for millennia.*

NICOLYA CHRISTI

THIRTEEN DIMENSIONS

As humans, we experience our reality in the material world of the third dimension. Vast legions of beings who exist in multidimensions overlight humanity and the Earth. These include: angels, archangels, ascended masters, higher intelligences, universal legions of light, spiritual teachers, guides, spiritually advanced civilizations, great councils of elders, interuniversals (highly evolved super-intelligent beings and energy forms that exist and travel between universes), extraterrestrials, star beings, and many more who guide the third dimension. These super-advanced intelligences channel new information to us, supporting and assisting us in our transformation to fifth-dimensional consciousness.

There are said to be twelve dimensional levels. However, a thirteenth-dimensional level is about to be brought into our awareness. My own guidance has revealed to me that there are a total of twenty-six dimensions. These are divided into two hemispheres within the universe. We are on the threshold of a shift from the southern to the northern galactic hemisphere; as this occurs we will reach the threshold of the thirteenth dimension, the rainbow bridge. In so doing we will begin to experience a whole new reality. As a result our consciousness will rapidly evolve. Imagine how the subtlest realignment of a satellite dish can allow us to pick up new information. Our consciousness is like a satellite, and as we shift into a new galactic hemisphere, we too will be on the receiving end of new information. First, we need to fully integrate the energies of the remaining dimensions into our consciousness, a process that may take little or much time, depending on the spiritual development of the individual.

Fundamental to this process is the clearing and healing of the human aura, which holds all trauma imprints. As we clear the aura we begin to activate the light-body and as we do so, like individual satellite receivers, we begin to align with higher and higher dimensions until we can resonate with the thirteenth, at which time we will have evolved into the prophesied state of *Homo luminous.**

---

*To understand more about the luminous energy field I recommend Alberto Villoldo's DVD, *Healing the Luminous Body: The Way of the Shaman.*

CLEARING TRAUMA IMPRINTS

Cast your mind back, if you will, to the Apollo 11 moon landing of 1969 and the statement made famous by Neil Armstrong, "One small step for man. One giant leap for mankind." Beginning to activate the light-body is a small but profoundly significant step, yet what this achieves is extraordinarily transformative, at both an individual and planetary level. In order for us to begin to engage with the process of evolving from *Homo sapiens* to *Homo luminous,* we must first seek to clear and heal the aura, which is the location of all held trauma. In so doing, we increase our ability to receive and hold spiritual light, which dramatically enhances our capacity for hypercommunication. As more of us connect to the higher realms, we begin to support the transmutation of the Earth into a true reflection of heaven.

To elevate our consciousness, which in turn will raise our vibration, we must seek to heal the trauma that prevents our liberation from suffering. Through countless incarnations the soul has borne witness to trauma. Everything we have ever experienced is stored in our soul's memory and registered deep within our cellular memory and our DNA including: victimization, persecution, oppression, abuse, control, manipulation, violence, illness, torture, suffering, emotional trauma, mental cruelty, spiritual repression, and so on. All of these have left core trauma imprints in the aura. Trauma imprints are the cause of physical, emotional, and mental imbalance. Since it is the information held within the luminous energy field that is the *cause* of illness, we need to focus our awareness on the "energetic," not the "molecular," if we are to heal and transcend dis-ease.

THE SOUL'S CHOICES

Here in the West, we believe that our predisposition to illness, the way we die, and mental and emotional imbalances are encoded in our genes and that we "inherit" the challenging difficulties experienced by our ancestors by incarnating into our family lineage. The medical establishment states that dis-ease originates from predisposed genetics. When we do not have conscious awareness, we can manifest genetic dis-ease. We are conditioned to believe this to be the case, so we allow our psyche to instruct our cells to create it. We believe that we are powerless when it comes to transcending the patterns of the past or the future. This is not so.

Of course, it is not by chance that we incarnate into an ancestral line that has a specific set of patterns for us to transcend. We do so, not to be marked for life by a predisposition, but in order to accomplish the particular healing required by incarnating into that specific group and so setting up the perfect and necessary conditions for our own healing in this lifetime. The soul chooses to incarnate into the circumstances most conducive for its growth, healing, and evolution.

The belief that we have a predisposition for certain experiences is accurate. We carry core trauma imprints forward from previous lives, where they lodge in the luminous energy field and remain until we reach a level of awareness that makes it possible to clear the origins of these traumas.

If there is a history of illness in your family lineage ask yourself "What is this teaching me about myself?" Recognize that by having chosen a family with health issues, you are on a learning curve of self-healing. Let us imagine that there is a history of stroke in the family. You may choose to work with that from a dietary and psychospiritual level in order to understand the lesson afforded you by becoming more self-aware. Or there may have been a history of mental instability in the family for many generations. Recognize that by exploring your mental attitude and seeking to gain mastery over it, you can alter your brain chemistry and transcend such a predisposition. If there is a history of abuse in your family, inner exploration at a physical, emotional, mental, and soul level will support your own healing and help you to understand and break free from the family pattern. Cultivate presence and commitment when it comes to your own psychological healing. Remind yourself that you have a body, feelings, and a mind but *you* are not any of these. These are a *part* of you, but they are not you.

If there is a history of addiction in your family or you are caught in addiction, recognize that you may have chosen to experience this in order to release yourself from a past or future life addiction, to heal a pattern of addiction, or to learn about it in order to help others heal. Addictions can operate at the subtlest levels and are not just physical. They can equally be emotional, mental, and psychological, as well as spiritual. Ask yourself, "For what purpose?" "How does it serve me to have this addiction?" Trust that your soul has chosen the experience and that there is a higher purpose involved; once you understand what that is, you can begin to heal what lies behind the addiction.

Healing the Ancestral Wound

There is another reason why we may choose to incarnate with a specific life pattern or predisposition. That is for the healing of an ancestral wound. Healing the ancestral wound is essential if we wish to liberate previous generations, our living relatives, and those who will succeed us. If we do not heal our ancestors then the patterns inherited from generations for hundreds, if not thousands of years, will continue.

So what can you do to heal your ancestors? First of all heal them by *remembering* them, not for the hurt they may have caused you, which keeps them bound to you and results in the experience of you continuing to experience their pain in your life, but by elevating them in your thoughts. Be willing to remember them as *they would wish* to be remembered. Honor that all you experienced by knowing them was for your higher good and served the ongoing evolution of your soul. Try to forgive them by showing compassion, empathy, and understanding, for in doing so you not only set them free, but also liberate yourself. Set an intent that "it ends here." Do this, not just for yourself or those who are no longer here, but for the generations to come. You can set a precedent for a future family lineage that is free from the bonds and chains of the patterns of the past. Just as we will often look to our ancestors for support, guidance, and the way forward, so too do they look to us for the same.

Within most families there tends to be an individual who is misunderstood or even ostracized. However, this member of the clan may well be an advanced soul who has chosen that particular family situation to clear and heal the ancestral wound. Because of the times we live in, the speed at which we can bring about transformational healing has accelerated and is now possible in a myriad of ways. Do you ever feel like the one who is different in your family? Do you feel as if the life you live and the values you live by differ vastly from your family? Do you feel that your family does not understand who you are? Do you find it a challenge to be with your family, feeling you have very little in common? If this is the case, it might be that, at a soul level, you have chosen to heal the ancestral wound, even if that is by acting as an antagonist who rattles the ancestral cage in which the wound is locked. This does not suggest you are a more "advanced" soul than your family members; it merely highlights that you carry a different soul energy. Incarnating into your family group also serves to focus your awareness on the healing and evolution of your own soul.

Your role in the family also may serve to clear ancestral karma, which usually entails direct experience of whatever it is, such as poverty, illness, abuse, and so on. Your decision to do this is noble and courageous. Rest assured that even if your family is unable to recognize your contribution in this life, they will do so when you reunite in Spirit. It is a sign of our personal holistic integration when we are aware of the contributions that we make to serve the highest good of others, yet remain humble about the opportunity to have done so. Let us also note that there is always an equal exchange and that even if it is not clear to you how your family has served the growth and healing of your own soul, you will know, either in this life or when you leave your body and return Home (to the higher dimensions).

The belief that we have a predisposition for certain experiences is accurate. We carry core trauma imprints forward from previous lives, where they lodge in the luminous energy field and remain there until we reach a level of awareness that makes it possible to clear the origins of these traumas. We do not inherit family patterns and predispositions, we *choose* them before we incarnate, the purpose being the healing and evolution of our soul. However, we forget this and become conditioned by the belief systems of a society and culture that has been locked into third-dimensional mentality for thousands of years. This results in a limited understanding of our soul purpose. As we begin to clear and heal the origins of our trauma it is necessary we become mindful and take full responsibility for the circumstances of our lives. We must let go of blame and shame and instead acknowledge that, at soul level, we each chose the conditions we endure or experience.

Only when we have understood this soul choice, have taken responsibility, and have acknowledged that our own psychospiritual wounds originated long before we encountered the people we are connected with by blood or friendship in this life, can we truly start to forgive ourselves and others. Only then do we come to recognize that those we viewed as "antagonists," are in fact among our greatest healers. We refrain from a tendency to apportion blame and judgment. We let go of resentment and sorrow and instead we are filled with gratitude and appreciation, which inspires us to act with loving-kindness. Ultimately, we will come to bless those who we may otherwise have judged to be the cause of our suffering, for these encounters have brought to us the gift of healing. When we feel continually blessed we *know* then that the origins of our personal trauma, as well as the ancestral wound, have been healed.

When focusing on healing the ancestral wound we need to recognize that we incarnate as "soul groups." We contract while in the higher realms to reincarnate as members of the same family. Some of our friends also fall into this soul group. Soul groups often incarnate together for many lifetimes and carry similar unhealed issues. By healing the karma between our family and friends, the individual soul is released from incarnating with that specific group again. When we are released from the family dynamics that have served our healing at a particular level, we become free to incarnate with a different group of souls. This is similar to graduating to the next level when in school or training and meeting groups of people with whom you form new friendships and have new experiences. We can also "graduate" to the next level while in the same life, when our karma is completed and we begin to attract a new soul group on Earth.

Soul Fragments

The luminous energy field is an information field. As the soul progresses through each incarnation, a part of it can become so increasingly traumatized that it fragments. Having lived countless lives across time, we leave behind these soul fragments in other parts of the world, which may explain why we often feel inexplicably drawn to foreign lands. This may be for the purpose of retrieving a soul fragment left behind after a traumatic past life experience. When we work with soul retrieval it is possible to "journey," from a visualization perspective, to specific locations around the world (and beyond) to retrieve these fragmented parts. We carry unhealed trauma into each life and it may take many lives before we are ready to heal these. Great expanses of time may be necessary in order for us to gain enough "energetic" distance from intensely traumatic experiences we have had in other lifetimes. Many are now reaching a point in their evolution where they now feel sufficiently strong, centered, and integrated enough to fully release core trauma imprints.

By clearing and healing accumulated trauma imprints we accelerate our spiritual evolution, freeing ourselves from physical, emotional, and mental patterns that do not serve the authentic Self. We become inspired— *in-spirito*. To activate the light-body we need to dissolve and heal all trauma imprints from the luminous energy field. So how can we do this?

CURING OR HEALING?

The medical profession diagnoses and offers prognosis at a physical level only. Medicine seeks to "cure" and uses "war" vocabulary such as "She's got a battle on her hands" or "He needs to fight it," "She's fighting to the death," or "We have to win this battle against cancer," and so on. We too take on this attitude and tell ourselves and each other: "I'll fight it," "I'll get rid of it," "It won't beat me," and so forth. Our own language and attitude is one of violence toward ourselves. We split off the part of us that is unwell, as if it were the enemy instead of the teacher and healer that it truly is.

We give away our power to self-heal and hand our lives over to an external source that lacks the resources or understanding to explore our dis-ease at a deeper or multidimensional level. Our brain and biochemistry alter and respond to our vocabulary, both to the words and the energy that our words convey. To understand the influence and impact of the words we use we need only look at the groundbreaking research carried out by Dr. Masaru Emoto, mentioned in chapter ten.

The approach of Western medicine is a reactive one. In terms of patient care the medical establishment is focused on "today" and the immediate future, failing to recognize that by merely treating the physical symptoms, the best it can offer is a "cure." However, the human being is multidimensional and the predispositions in the luminous energy field, created in the past or future, far outweigh any present causal factors of disease.

Often, despite a "remission" or a "cure," it is only a matter of time before the ailment resurfaces. The reason for this is because the *cause* of the illness remains unaddressed. Adept healers, most noticeably shamanic healers, seek not to cure but to *heal*. They can assist us to approach dis-ease from an entirely different perspective, one that treats the human being holistically, as a mind, a body, a soul, a spirit, a psyche, and emotionally, mentally, psychologically, energetically, karmically, spiritually, and multidimensionally. This method of healing invites us to step out of time and to move into a heightened state of awareness, an altered state of consciousness, in order to initiate healing at a core level.

When we are "cured" we are not "healed" and invariably what ails us will return. Skilled healers, many trained as shamans, understand the importance of a *sacred space* for healing and know that much of the healing required by humans is undertaken by higher-dimensional intelligences. The human body vibrates at a slow frequency on the third-dimensional level. To induce a *healing* we must create an appropriate energetic space to allow the higher vibrating multidimensional energies to assist in the process.

A "sacred space" can be created in a variety of ways. Shamans call in *the four directions,* and *above and below,* which they refer to as the domain of the "eco-sphere." All competent healers seek to raise the vibration of the space they use for treatment. Chants and incantations, prayers and mantras, singing and toning, burning oil and incense, lighting candles and playing healing music all raise the vibration and help to create a sacred ambience and a safe space. It is a prerequisite that we create a sacred space within and around ourselves so that spirit helpers, in the higher dimensions, can assist us to heal. If we fail to create a conducive environment, although it may be possible to achieve a spontaneous cure, it is likely that the illness will return, as we will not be working at a core level with the *cause* and the trauma imprint origin, nor will we be gaining the assistance of unseen helpers required for a healing.

Illness allows us to rebalance karma and heal soul trauma held within our cellular memory. It is also a great teacher for mastering our thoughts and emotions, which can and do make us ill. However, it is important to mention that in some cases of illness and dis-ease, it is our soul's plan to experience this process as a means of leaving our bodies. Sometimes the soul's process is one of clearing and healing at many levels through a terminal illness. Once this has occurred we no longer need to remain in this life, but instead can cross over into the higher realms, review the life we have just lived, and choose to incarnate into a different set of circumstances altogether.

The origins of trauma imprints span many lifetimes and are triggered by specific experiences we attract into this life. We may have been physically or emotionally abandoned as children. We may have been abused, humiliated, frightened or threatened by the behavior or expectations of those we encountered. Past and future life issues also remain lodged within the luminous energy field, as can the trauma imprints of discarnate spirits who may be attached to us. We need to work with a highly developed, competent, and skilled healer who can act as a bridge for us between the visible and invisible worlds.

An important question to consider is: "What is the purpose of this physical dis-ease?" To work toward core healing we need to question ourselves. How does it serve us to experience illness or imbalance? What does it teach us about ourselves? What is its gift? If we fail to learn the meaning and purpose of the illness, we may well find a temporary cure, but not a healing. To create the perfect inner and outer environment that will allow us to explore, clear, and heal the origins of our trauma requires our emotional intelligence. We do not need to engage the mind; we have only to invoke the wisdom of the body. There is a higher purpose for ALL of our experiences and the body understands this well, even if the mind struggles with this as a concept.

The esoteric approach to illness, such as the examples I speak of below, make permanent *healing* a possibility. Dis-ease or a specific malady will not return as long as the recipient remains attuned to the elevated state of consciousness that initiated the healing. A recurrence may occur if a part of your soul journey is to experience such again in order to burn off deeper layers of karma and initiate further soul healing.

There are many healing practices and therapies available to us now that can help accelerate our path to wholeness and integration. Listed below are just a few of the options that will support us to heal the body, emotions, mind, energy, psyche, and soul. (Please see the resource directory for a more complete listing.)

For any healing to occur, a feeling of safety is singularly the most important factor. Both safety in the environment and safety borne out of trust in the person facilitating the healing process. If you wish to measure how effective your chosen healing method is likely to be, you first need to monitor how "safe" you feel. This is not something you can assess with your mind, although it is essential to inquire about the qualifications of the healer has and how long he or she has been practicing.

Initially, meet with the healer to see how well you connect with each other and discuss what your needs are and if the healer is appropriate for you. Observe how the healer responds to you and your questions. Do you feel understood? Do you feel empathy and sensitivity? Does the healer appear confident? Do you sense they have integrity? Do you feel seen and heard? Does the healer appear fully present to you or somehow absent? Trust your feelings. When all of these elements are established, assess how the surrounding space feels to you. This is important. Do not be afraid to ask for another initial meeting. If you are still unsure, check how open the healer is to answer any further questions via a short telephone call or a succinct e-mail. Remember, depth healing can never be achieved if you do not feel totally safe. It is best to choose someone who is highly recommended or has a good reputation.

Psychotherapeutic Practices

The two most poisonous emotions we can experience are *fear* and *anger*. When we experience these or another person is directing them toward us these emotions are received like a poison and can have a catastrophic effect on us. It is wise to ask ourselves why we are attracting these intrusive thought forms. By understanding that *like attracts like* and that something in our own emotional make up is inviting fear and anger, we realize that we have an opportunity to heal at a core level. Psychotherapeutic methods are enormously valuable to help our understanding of the "why's" and "how's" of our patterns, issues, and behaviors. They can prove invaluable when it comes to preparing the ground for us to work at an energetic and metaphysical level. These methods also help us to process and integrate the experiences that arise when we engage with more esoteric practices to heal the energy body and open to our multidimensionality.

Psychotherapy, birthed in the late nineteenth century by Sigmund

Freud, has served us well until recently. However, as our consciousness is now evolving so quickly, we need new methods for the rapid healing of our physical, emotional, and mental levels and energy bodies. Shamans view negative emotions as noxious darts that enter the luminous energy field and deposit their poisons. In a couple of sessions a skilled shamanic practitioner can clear what could ordinarily take psychotherapy years to accomplish. This is because the psychological approach, with its focus on the re-telling of past trauma, can re-traumatize the client; rather than resolving the trauma imprint, it causes it to become further embedded.

There is a fine line in psychotherapeutic practice between facilitating the healing of trauma and leaving the client further traumatized. It takes a great amount of skill and emotional intelligence for a therapist to create this fine balance. A highly sensitive and skilled psychotherapist will help us to understand the root of our suffering and difficult emotions. However, a common experience for clients is that, despite the insights gained into their behavioral patterns, fundamental issues can still remain, albeit to a far lesser degree. As a result of psychotherapy, we find that we become better equipped to manage difficult thoughts and emotions, yet core issues will often still arise. Working with the luminous energy field is essential if we are to heal core trauma.

Hypnosis

Hypnosis can prove an enormously successful healing method, as it induces delta waves (the brainwaves that are present for up to two years in infants) and theta waves. We function in theta from the ages of two to seven. This is the brain wave pattern of pre-waking and sleeping in adults. Theta waves register below alpha waves, which are the predominant brainwaves from the ages of seven to twelve. The theta wave induces the "hypnogogic" state associated with altered states of consciousness and enables us to access and reprogram the unconscious mind. Hypnosis is a powerful tool that allows us to bypass the left side of the brain and penetrate the right brain hemisphere, which can then lead to core healing and a transformation of consciousness.

Energy Psychology

Energy psychology targets the energy field and facilitates our ability to access the brain enabling it to receive "downloads" of information at phenomenal speeds. Energy psychology includes: EFT (emotional freedom technique), TFT (thought field therapy), EMDR (eye movement and desensitization reprocessing), and Psyche K (psychological kinesiology). These modalities allow the innate wisdom of the body to respond energetically to reprogram the unconscious. In as little as ten minutes, energy psychology can facilitate a release of self-limiting beliefs and fears that may have blocked us for decades. Most energy medicine practices consist of working with areas of the physical and energetic bodies. These include rapid eye movements, the tapping of specific meridian points, and muscle testing, all of which allow us access to the wisdom held within the physical and energetic bodies.

Energy psychology methods tend to bypass the rational mind and engage the abstract mind. An example of this can be seen in the story of an acquaintance who had been diagnosed with epilepsy from the age of seven and had been prescribed powerful drugs to control it. At the age of thirty, she decided to train as an EFT practitioner and began to work on her own condition. In a matter of weeks she had stopped taking the medication. Three years later she has not experienced a single fit, nor has she once had to revert back to medication. Another friend working with EFT has practically cleared her diabetic condition and has reduced her insulin medication by two thirds.

Shamanism

I would like to focus specifically on the healing methods of the shamans who have the greatest understanding of the luminous energy field. Some shamanic healing practices originating as long ago as 50,000 years are still available to us. Ancient shamanic wisdom speaks to "a Self that exists outside of time," a Self that "has never known illness or disease for these cannot touch it." These teachings tell us that no matter how much we may suffer on a physical level, at the same time there is always a part of us that is vibrant, whole, and consistently well.

The mind can serve as a hindrance or a great support for our self-healing. From a human perspective our quest for liberation and enlightenment requires that our mind is not a foe but an ally. Our thoughts have an enormous influence on our experience. A significant step that you can make in your journey to wholeness and integration is to become aware of the choices you can make with regard to what you think, what you dream into reality. When the shamans speak of a "Self that exists outside of time that has never known illness or disease" and "that there is a part of us that is always vibrant and whole," we can choose to accept this as a truth or dismiss such a concept. If we choose to align our thoughts with this, we will manifest it as a reality. However, if we deny this possibility, we deny ourselves an opportunity for transformation.

There are many books, CDs, and DVDs available on the topic of how our thoughts shape our reality. To explore this concept further, obtain a copy of *The Secret,* or *What the Bleep Do We Know!?* (available in both book and DVD format), a good place to begin to explore the power of the mind. We need to *change our minds,* if we truly wish to transform our lives.

SOUL RETRIEVAL AND THE
CLEARING OF ENTITIES OR INTRUSIVE ENERGIES

Two shamanic healing modalities that support the activation of the light-body are soul retrieval and the clearing of entities or intrusive energies. They offer specific ways to heal core trauma imprints. Soul retrieval is an integral shamanic healing practice used to clear the luminous energy field. It is a process in which the healer journeys with or on behalf of the client to recover a fragmented part of the soul that has been lost somewhere in time, usually in former lives. These lost parts of the soul have become "frozen in time," as a result of extreme trauma and pain experienced in specific former lives. Often, the sense of something missing, which many of us experience, is in fact a part of ourselves, soul fragments that we left behind many lifetimes ago. This is true for the majority of us until the time comes when we seek to retrieve these lost parts of ourselves. We need to retrieve these fragmented parts of the soul in order to clear trauma imprints lodged within the aura.

Even though various psychotherapeutic practices help to catalyze enormous changes within us, release much of the powerful emotional "charge" we carry, help us to understand the "why" of our emotional reactions, and offer us transformational insights and information, they are unable to assist us to reclaim soul fragments. For this we look to the mystical realm of healing, where the emphasis is on the energetic, astral, metaphysical, and esoteric—*the soul*. The role of the adept or shamanic healer is to *retrieve* lost soul fragments and return them to the psyche for integration by working with the abstract, the intangible, the non-physical, nonvisible realms. Shamanism is rooted in cyclical time where the past, present, and future are realities that occur simultaneously.

Soul retrieval can take two routes. The first is to journey along what is termed a "timeline" into the past to discover the original wound that lies at the root of the trauma we experience in our current lives, so we can transform it and heal. Every challenge or issue we face in this life is simply a replay of original psychospiritual wounds.

The second route of soul retrieval is to journey forward along the timeline for what is termed a "destiny retrieval," where you and the healer visit your "future Self" who is already healed. By working with the healer you are able to utilize the information from the healed future Self to effect changes in the present. This method is a relatively new healing tool in the West. Traveling forward in time to view our future lives gives us the opportunity to encounter and address our future Self and gain valuable, transformative information about our current situation from a perspective that ensures our healing. By visiting our healed future Self we are able to see all that we are becoming and this Self is able to share with us how we arrived at this point. We then have the advantage of working with this information to rapidly transform ourselves and our lives.

Let us now take a look at *entities* or *intrusive energies.* Whenever we are on the receiving end of negative thought forms our aura registers an intrusive energy. Dark thoughts and entities enter the body like *dark arrows,* depositing their toxic load into the physical system. This negative energy also impacts the psyche and embeds itself into the aura where it becomes crystallized. Negative thoughts from ourselves or others have an impact on our health and materialize as warts, boils, spots, fungus, cysts, blisters, tumors, hardening of the arteries, rashes, aches and pains, and so on. At a deeper, unconscious level we seem to know this. We make statements such as: "I feel like I've been stabbed in the back," "I'm sick and tired of," and so on. This offers some explanation as to why the medical industry can only manage or cure symptoms (which generally return), because the patient is being treated at a one-dimensional level.

We *know, sense, and feel* when another is thinking negatively about us or wishing us ill. This can result in illness as colds, flu, stomach upsets, or worse as the body attempts to throw off the energy that it experiences as negative or attacking. However, we only manifest physical reactions when we ourselves are feeling negative, as *like attracts like.* So we cannot apportion blame to others, as they serve only as a mirror for parts of ourselves. If we remained positive in our thoughts, speech, and actions we would no longer attract negative energy. If we did so our aura would be clear and strong enough to simply deflect intrusive energies. These would then rebound back to the sender who would continue to manifest physical symptoms of illness. It is not just the negative thoughts of others that make us unwell at a physical, emotional, or mental level. It is also our own that result in making us ill.

When I become upset by a situation, I pause and ask myself, "What is this mirroring to me?" "What does this show me about my behavior toward others or perhaps to myself?" The physical symptoms that arise as a result of intrusive energies are not separate from ascension symptoms; they are the same. Ultimately, ALL diagnosed and undiagnosed illness and ailments are a *transmutation* process through which

we redress karma, heal, refine, and transform ourselves, raise consciousness and vibration. When our vibration reaches a certain level, intrusive energies can no longer attach to or embed in our luminous energy
field.

Attachment and Possession

For millennia the term *entity/entities has* been used to describe discarnate souls, also known as *earthbound, disembodied spirits, ghosts,* or
apparitions. These terms describe those who once lived on Earth and
have failed to cross over successfully into the Spirit world. There are
several reasons why a soul can remain earthbound. For example, some
have experienced so much earthly happiness during their lives that they
remain attached to people and places. Some are afraid they will go
to hell as a result of religious indoctrination. Many have experienced
extreme suffering or have been impacted by tragedy, while others are
bound by pacts made with a loved one, such as "I'll never leave you."
Then there are those souls who are afraid to move on, understanding
how much grief their passing has caused. Others have unresolved issues
with the living, some may have passed in tragic circumstances or experienced a sudden death and do not feel ready to move on. The reasons
are many.

Discarnate spirits often seek out a family member who is either
sensitive, ill, psychic, or depressed to attach to. Most *attachments* are
benign, some feel lost (often children who have experienced a traumatic
death) and are drawn to warm and compassionate hosts. The main reason for attachments is that ultimately these disembodied spirits are seeking assistance and help from their hosts. They seek to free themselves
from the astral levels where they have become "stuck," so they can move
into higher levels and realms. I am reminded of a friend who reported
that each time he went for a walk down a particular country lane he
had an eerie sense of being watched. This increased to the point where
he was able to visualize a little girl dressed in a Victorian dress clutch-
ing a teddy. I advised him that when he saw her next to telepathically

encourage her to "go toward the light," which he did. Several years later, when having a reading with a medium, he was told of a "little girl who was close to him because he had "helped her." The medium told him that the little girl was saying "thank you" to him. At the time he could not place who she was, as he does not have children or know of anyone with a young girl he had helped who had subsequently passed over. Only after the reading did he remember the encounter on the country lane. Clearly this little girl did not attach to him, but had recognized his sensitivity and thought that he might help her.

A disembodied spirit may be looking for a way to continue the life they once lived and the host may experience a dramatic change in lifestyle by suddenly finding themselves frequenting a pub, a betting office, or pursuing a life that observers may comment on as being "totally out of character." Once an understanding is reached concerning the purpose of an attachment, the discarnate spirit needs to be encouraged to cross the threshold from this world to the next. Energetic intervention with a great degree of love and compassion is required to help entities cross into the realm of Spirit. No pharmaceutical drugs, medicines, psychotherapy, or psychiatry will resolve the issue of entity attachment.

It is estimated that a large percentage of the human population has experienced an attachment at some point in their lives. We do not always have to consult a professional to release such attachments, as merely by raising our consciousness, we raise our vibration, at which point the entity will leave, as entities can only attach to a low vibrational energy field (aura). Raising our consciousness requires us to think and feel differently, to be more positive and to be willing to let go of our negative thoughts. We need to explore our attachment to thinking and feeling negatively and ask ourselves, "How does it serve me?" for at some level it does. If we can understand that a negative view of ourselves, other people, or the world, is usually because a part of us is in fear or pain, we can begin to change our perception and experience. This in turn alters our vibration and can automatically release an attachment, which could change our life.

There is also a rarer type of entity that can invade a human being, one that is far more sinister than an attachment and is identified as a *possession*. These entities often come from lower vibrating worlds; in other words they are nonhuman. These are "dark entities" whose light has become diminished following many cycles of negativity, as they roam the lower levels of the astral plane (see glossary) preying on souls in that dimension, as well as this one. Possessions are low frequency entities who literally invade (as opposed to attach) and prey on particularly sensitive people or those who are emotionally, mentally, or physically unwell. They attach themselves to people, as well as to properties and locations, affecting those who reside in or visit such places. At the very least, dark entities will influence the behavior, emotions, thought patterns, and health of those who are vulnerable to them. At worst, they can completely take over a life, controlling behavior and infiltrating the body, emotions, and mind. The recipient of a dark entity can become a shadow of their former self. Friends and family notice extreme mood swings, bouts of aggression and violence, as well as self-destructive tendencies. Those afflicted usually become ill, weak, depressed, anti-social, suicidal, unpredictable, and even "schizophrenic."

Possessions have been recorded throughout history. Attachments are relatively unknown in the Western world. However, the concept is well known and documented in many Eastern traditions and indigenous tribes and cultures. Unlike the destructive, violent, and terrifying experience of possession, the impact of an attachment is far more benign, often resulting in dysfunctional behavior such as addiction, self-sabotage, fearfulness, sadness, various health issues, or chronic fatigue, which goes unnoticed, as our culture accepts such as normal modes of behavior, usually labeling them as "depression."

Most attachments occur during a moment of trauma, often in childhood or when we are vulnerable or ill. Hospitals, psychiatric institutions, and prisons play host to many attachments, as do churches and places of history, where wars, persecutions, and trauma remain alive in the energetic memory of a place. Attachments will often gravitate toward those with an addiction to drugs, sex, or alcohol, or those who are "depressed." Possession, on the other hand, occurs as a result of being in a severely low mental state, where there is a marked sensitivity, or when we are very ill and alone without the protective shield that love can provide.

In the past possession has been treated aggressively by priests who wave crucifixes and recite specific passages from the Bible. However, as the collective consciousness begins to shift and our understanding becomes more humanitarian, we begin to recognize that we can approach possession and entity attachment in a very different way, one that respects both the host and the attachment or dark entity. Now, instead of using traditional exorcism, a new breed of specialists are responding. These include Ian Lawman (*Living with the Dead*/Living TV), a leading UK specialist, who adopts an attitude of authority, but also uses sensitivity and understanding, respect and skill, wisdom and spiritual awareness.

Most discarnate spirits attach themselves to relatives. Earthbound spirits are drawn to the most sensitive or vulnerable in the family, even if they had no close relationship with that family member while living. Indigenous cultures protect their young and newborns from "dark forces" by using specific talismans, incantations, and the burning of specific oils and incense. To many Westerners, such practices appear theatrical or primitive, yet these indigenous cultures display a natural wisdom that far exceeds the understanding of the modern world.

We need only look at the lack of crime and addictions within these cultures and observe how these people live with love and in joy to recognize that something about their culture and people is different. Very few attachments or possessions are evident in Eastern countries. If they do occur, immediate action is taken to address the situation. Tibetan, Peruvian, and various indigenous peoples of the world remain alert and responsive to the reality of attachments and possessions. In Thailand, mini-temples are erected and dedicated to appease and honor those souls who remain caught between the realms. Our Eastern cousins honor discarnate souls, think well of them, and acknowledge them as a part of the fabric of their earthly life. Perhaps this is why attachments and possessions are not the issue they are in Western cultures.

Often earthbound spirits are drawn to friends or family members because they fail to realize they have passed over and therefore take up residence with the family again. Discarnate spirits believe they are still alive and *are* the person whose body they are operating through. For example, a loving grandmother who has died might want to protect a vulnerable grandchild and will attach to it. The grandmother does not realize she is no longer living and only wishes to remain with the family. She is caught in the astral plane, the place between the physical and spiritual planes, inhabited by discarnate souls, who many of us encounter in our dreams.

The astral plane is the realm containing the memories of our life. The discarnate soul *embodies* a living human form to continue the experience of physical life, which feels as real to them as when they were actually alive. So the grandmother, for example, continues living as she once did, believing she is visiting her grandchild who is alive in a body. By the time the child becomes an adult (attachments can remain with their hosts for lifetimes), the grandmother has become so used to living through her host that she forgets she is experiencing life through another body and begins to "take over" believing the body is hers and the host is the attachment. This is not the same as possession by a "dark" entity, which is dangerous for the physical, emotional, and mental health of the victim. Some dark entities have never had a human life, while others were a negative force when inhabiting a body.

To experience an attachment is ultimately detrimental to the host, as the thoughts and behaviorisms of the discarnate spirit begin to control those of the person to whom they are attached. Edith Fiorre, one of the world's leading experts on entity attachment, has hundreds of documented case studies of different types of attachment and the impact they have on a person's life. Fiorre shares an example of an eminent male professor, happily married with children, who suddenly became overwhelmed with an urge to cross dress. This escalated to the point where he felt compelled to consider a transgender operation to become a woman. This man, by chance, heard of Fiorre at the same time he was about to embark upon transgender counseling to prepare for the operation. He arrived at the session with her in a traumatized state, as the compulsion to become a woman was too strong to overcome, yet to proceed would mean the loss of his wife, children, and career. During the course of the first session he discovered a female attachment who proved to be the cause of his anguish. It transpired that the female discarnate soul had no idea she was not alive and only wished to continue to live her life. Following several sessions with Fiorre, the discarnate female spirit was guided back to the light and no longer continued as a disembodied spirit. Consequently, the professor called off the operation and is once again living a successful and fulfilled life as a married man with children, but has developed a greater understanding of the unseen influences that are all around us, ones that our indigenous cousins find as natural as the air they breathe.

Fiorre cites several cases where an addiction does not belong to the host, but to the attached entity. By removing the attachment, behavior that had been out of character for the host disappears. Often someone with an addiction will try to do everything to overcome it but without success. What is not understood is that the problem of the attachment needs to be addressed. It is important to acknowledge that we can only attract an attachment or a possession if something within us has rendered us vulnerable in the first place.

Over time the host of the attachment (or possession) assumes the character, mannerisms, preferences, and behavioral patterns of the discarnate spirit. Entities influence the thoughts and emotions of their hosts, who also take on the cravings or addictions of their attachment. For example, a normally quiet and studious person may suddenly become the life of the party. Someone who has been averse to drugs may become an addict. A nonsmoker may get an overpowering urge to suddenly take up smoking. A celibate may become a sexual predator. Similarly, such phenomena can also occur with recipients of organ transplants. It not uncommon for a teetotaler who has received the liver of someone who liked alcohol to find themselves starting to drink or a classical music fan who doesn't drive, in accordance with the tastes of the organ donor, to develop a passion for rock music and Harley Davidsons! This may occur because the recipient is picking up the memory traces stored in the donated organ (scientists have now discovered that the main organs of the body contain brain cells) or because the donor is attaching to the recipient.

The most likely cause of attachment and possession is *negative thinking,* although illness, deep unhealed trauma, and hypersensitivity can also attract them. To ensure against this, it is necessary to monitor your thoughts and remain mindful of the impact they have, not only on yourself, but also those around you. It is easy to recognize a detrimental thought, as the instant you think it you will feel the effect in your body. A mantra you may find helpful is, "If it does not uplift me, I do not think it." This can also apply to what you do, who you spend time with, and to other areas of your life. If it does not uplift you, then do not do it! When we permanently think uplifting thoughts our vibration is raised to a sufficiently high frequency and disembodied spirits and entities are unable to attach to us.

During my many years of working psychospiritually in client practice, I have come across cases of entity attachment. Possessions are extremely rare and require the help of an expert medium who specializes in working with darker forces, as clearing them can be dangerous to both the host and the healer.

There are various ways to remove an attachment in a way that is both respectful and loving. Consulting someone in the spiritualist church who is proficient at doing so is one option. Working with a reputable and experienced shaman is another. Approaching a hypnotherapist who specializes in entity attachment can also be effective. However, whether we continue to attract discarnate spirits is dependent on our understanding that there is an imbalance within us that was responsible for the original attachment.

An insurance policy against attachment or possession is to raise our level of consciousness and therefore our rate of vibration. We can begin this process with our thoughts, by *changing our minds,* by choosing to view ourselves, other people, and life in general, through a different lens, one that has a softer, more loving focus. We need to be willing to take responsibility for everything that has happened to us from the moment of our birth to our final breath. We must remember that our soul has chosen all experiences from past to present for the purpose of balancing karma and to continue with its evolutionary journey. Our perceived adversaries are, from the perspective of our soul, our staunch allies, loyally engaged in their part of the soul contract we agreed upon before incarnation. When we realize this fact, our perception is changed forever and we view ourselves, other people, and our lives very differently. We eliminate all thoughts of blame and begin to believe that we can transform our lives, once we realize that "bad" things are not happening to us, that we are not victims, but that we have chosen these relationships for the healing and growth of our own soul.

Shamanic healing can remove attachments quickly and effectively. However, the client has to be willing to acknowledge their part in how they came to host an entity in the first place, due to the unhealed places within them that resulted in a lowered vibration. Often an attachment occurs in childhood when a substantial trauma has been experienced. The more vulnerable, hurt, and lonely we feel, the more chance there is of an attachment occurring. Those with an addiction to alcohol, drugs, or sex are literally rendered "wide open" for attachment, commonly attracting discarnates who experienced the very same addictions when alive in the physical, who then exacerbate the addictions of their host. It is common to have more than one attachment.

An Example from My Client Practice

I would like share an example of entity attachment from my client practice. For confidentiality I shall refer to the client as "Peter."

Peter struck me as a deep and sensitive soul. He followed a vegan diet, was very soft spoken, with a marked air of calm about him. The man who sat in front of me appeared composed, intelligent, philosophical, and aware of his spirituality. At the commencement of the session he made it very clear that he was no longer willing to continue with his lifestyle as it was and declared that he now felt ready to understand what lay at the root of the pain he knew to be inside of him.

Peter explained that he had thought he would have drunk himself to death by the time he was thirty and how shocked he was to wake on the morning of his thirtieth birthday. From the age of twenty he began to drink alcohol, take drugs, and smoke cigarettes. Until that time, however, he had had no desire to do these things. Peter further explained how very sensitive he had been as a child and how this, together with his gentleness, had resulted in difficulties at home and in the world, where he felt misjudged and misunderstood. At the age of nineteen he experienced a painful trauma and it was a few months afterward that he started to drink. When he did so he felt different, had more confidence, and for the first time in his life he became outgoing and began to create a social circle. People behaved differently toward him when he was drinking or taking drugs. He felt accepted and able to socialize without the crippling shyness that had led to him to be so withdrawn before his drinking began. Once he started to drink and take drugs, he lost control of his life and as a result his twenties remained a blur.

Peter had many brushes with death as a result of his alcohol and drug taking. He drank throughout each day and night, ingesting copious amounts of drugs at the same time. Throughout his twenties and early thirties his job was to manage catering establishments. He spent eighteen hours a day working, drinking, and taking drugs. Peter remained single, unable to allow anyone to get too close. He confided in me that he would cringe at the thought of any physical contact, even avoiding a customary greeting or a goodbye. He rejected intimacy of any kind. However, he engaged in casual sex and dysfunctional sexual stimulation. Because of his job he was surrounded by people for eighteen hours plus a day, but during the remaining hours he lived in virtual isolation, shut away inside of himself.

He explained how excruciatingly difficult it was for him to even consider trusting anyone and how much fear accompanied relating to others. He shared how deeply suspicious he was of other people's motives. He felt he was split in two, being the center of attention (he was well liked by both work colleagues and customers) when drinking and taking drugs, but living like a recluse, even suspicious of his housemates, when he was not working.

Aged thirty-two, Peter became involved with a woman and attempted to maintain a long distance relationship, which suited his need for emotional and physical distance. He would meet this woman twice a month and found that when he was with her a part of him was beginning to open to emotional intimacy. When they were apart, however, he chose to have virtually no contact with her. Eventually she issued an ultimatum. Either they take the relationship to the next level or it would have to finish. Peter made the choice of committing to the relationship, which meant leaving his job and the city he lived and worked in to move to a coastal town with a slower pace of life. On the eve of leaving the city to start his new life, in another drunken state, he spent the night in the bed of a stranger. Within days of moving to be with his partner, this infidelity and several others came to light.

During the weeks that followed the relationship became a "confessional," as Peter poured out his life story to his partner, returning to his childhood when a devastating sexually abusive experience had occurred. Peter surrendered to the relationship and allowed himself to release the burden he had been carrying for many years. He began to "breakdown" in order to "breakthrough," a process that would take several months as he disassembled himself before piecing himself back together again.

Peter had been filled with self-loathing since that early childhood experience. When I first encountered him, his energy field was grey and closely compressed to his body. During his "breakdown" period I witnessed an "entity" leaving his body and energy field. It was a vivid experience. Suddenly, midsentence, Peter began to violently shake and became ice cold. I wrapped him in blankets and gave him a hot drink, but to no avail. Covered with layers of blankets and with the heating full on, he was still unable to control the shaking and sensation of ice coldness. He became aware of a cackling, laughing sound and could hear a voice mocking and goading him. He described a vision of a malicious face in front of him, taunting and laughing hysterically at him. I knew what was occurring. He was experiencing an entity release, which happens when an attachment is no longer able to hold on to the person once their vibration has risen to a high enough level.

For Peter, the commitment of the work he had undertaken to explore his issues and the release of his feelings had served to raise his vibration and dislodged the attachment. This entity was not a relative but a discarnate spirit, probably picked up in one of the many drinking establishments (a common place for an attachment to occur) he had frequented or worked in. Peter remained ice cold for several hours following this experience and shaken for a day or two, after which he reported a profound sense of relief, "as if a weight had been lifted." He found that his desire for alcohol literally disappeared overnight. All that remained was the mental pattern, which he began working on to clear. Even though his habitual mind encouraged the pattern and routine of drinking, his physical body had no desire to respond. From that point onward he no longer drank alcohol.

Peter's dysfunctional behavior and self-destructive tendencies were beginning to heal. He changed his job so he was no longer surrounded by alcohol and drugs and instead began to paint, realizing a talent he had long been aware of and yet had been unable to express. He embarked upon a vocation as an artist and began to make changes in his life. However, after a couple of years, when faced with stressful situations, he became aware that the desire to have a drink was resurfacing. This was not nearly as strong as before, but he was aware of it coming into his thoughts and he decided to investigate. He also realized that there was an aspect of the sexual dysfunction issue he could not clear despite the psychological awareness he had gained and the physical, emotional, and mental healing he had undergone.

During a period when Peter was reflecting on these remaining issues of alcohol and sexual dysfunction, he produced a painting that he described as "coming out of nowhere." He felt that both the painting and the title *The Ancestral Wound* had been "channeled." Peter showed me the painting, which depicts him sitting in the center of the image with a host of faceless "energies" surrounding him. He shared how, when he finished painting the image, it immediately dawned on him that these "energies" were his male ancestors asking him to heal the ancestral male pattern. At this point he became aware that the spirit of his grandfather was with him. Peter intuitively felt that his grandfather was living through him in order to help him heal the male lineage from patterns of abuse and alcohol dependency that had existed for generations. Peter responded to this feeling and worked consciously and with dedication to heal this wound.

As we worked together it came to light that Peter's grandfather, who he knew very little about, had died of alcoholism and had issues around abuse. Peter had always been the "sensitive" one in the family and he felt it was possible that his grandfather had attached to him in his early childhood, at the time of the sexual abuse incident, which had proved to be a defining moment of his own life, at just six years of age. After this, his character had undergone a marked change. He retreated inside of himself, becoming overly shy, reserved, and isolated, and began the descent into a dark cocoon of self-loathing.

We worked with "spirit-releasement" techniques (see resource directory) and discovered that indeed his disembodied grandfather was attached to him. As is often the case with an attachment, releasing his grandfather was a gentle and simple process. Since then, Peter's issues of alcohol addiction and abuse have cleared. After some "reprogramming" and self-discipline on Peter's part to break the established residual mental patterns, the physical and energetic connection was severed when his grandfather's spirit moved into the light.

Five years later Peter is happy to report that he rarely drinks alcohol.

He perhaps has one or two beers every few months solely for social pleasure, but experiences no need to do so. His relationship to sexuality has become healthy and functional. His career as an artist is going from strength to strength and he describes his inspiration as being from a "higher source," feeling that his work is guided and partly channeled as a means to serve humanity.

SELF-RESPONSIBILITY FOR OUR FUTURE LIFE EXPERIENCES

In the long term we need to be mindful of and take responsibility for our own well-being and balance. If we were to physically detox and then immediately follow this by ingesting vast quantities of chips, sweets, coffee, alcohol, and cakes, we would experience a toxic overload and resulting ill health. The same can be said for the energy field. Once we have cleared it, we need to keep it clear of further imprints. For our aura to remain clear we need to observe ourselves under a magnifying glass, leaving no stone unturned and no dark corner unexplored in our quest for the healing and resolution of trauma imprints that may re-imprint the luminous energy field.

In the same way that a lower vibrating energy field attracts a low vibrating energy, a higher vibrating energy field attracts higher vibrating energies. How wonderful to have an angel as an attachment! For this is perfectly feasible and happens all the time.

TWENTY-ONE ARROWS: A MAP FOR EVOLVING CONSCIOUSNESS

Native American medicine teachings have a map for evolving consciousness, which consists of *seven dark, seven light,* and *seven rainbow arrows.* They offer a wonderful, succinct summary of how we proceed. All twenty-one arrows, whether they are rainbow, light, or dark, are aspects within us. They teach us about ourselves. All that we experience externally is an opportunity for us to turn our attention inward and question the messages we are receiving about ourselves through either the reactions or responses from the environment.

Each dark arrow is a "hook," which acts as a magnet for entities and intrusive energies. Realize also that we can inflict any one of these arrows upon ourselves. We tend to project our own dark arrows into the environment, which then mirrors to us our own projections.

The Seven Dark Arrows are:
- Attachment
- Dependency
- Judgment
- Comparison
- Expectation
- The Needy Child Syndrome
- Self-Importance (ego)

As we are aware, *like attracts like*. When we find ourselves on the receiving end of a dark arrow, whether it is self-inflicted or arrives via another, we need to be aware that something within us has magnetized this experience toward us. So, for example, we may feel upset if we find ourselves being compared to another, which is a judgment. It is necessary for us to acknowledge why we feel this way. It may be that we ourselves compare and judge or that we self-judge, comparing aspects of ourselves to others. The fact is that anything we attract is teaching us something about ourselves.

The Seven Light Arrows are:
- Self-Awareness
- Self-Appreciation
- Self-Acceptance
- Self-Pleasure
- Self-Love

- Self-Actualization
- Impeccability (always doing the best you can whenever you can, and if you could do better you would).

The Seven Rainbow Arrows are:
- Illumination
- Introspection
- Trust and Innocence
- Wisdom
- Open Heart-to-Heart Communication
- Balance of Male and Female Energies
- Abundance and Prosperity

When we have mastered the art of the fourteen light and rainbow arrows we will have transformed our third-dimensional consciousness to a fifth-dimensional one. When our luminous energy field is imprinted with trauma, not only are we vulnerable to the impact of negative external stimuli, but our physical bodies are weakened because of the aura's absorption of the energy we are attracting to ourselves. When we are clear of trauma imprints we dwell in a place of deep peace and harmony within ourselves. Our immune system will maintain a state of optimum health and we will greatly develop our capacity for empathy and compassion. We will consistently feel centered and in a state of equilibrium with a refined sensitivity and renewed enthusiasm for life. The Native Americans say that for every dark arrow we break we automatically receive a light one, and that for every light arrow integrated, we earn a rainbow arrow. Once we have mastered the level of the rainbow arrows, we have achieved mastery over the body, emotions, and mind. We become Self-actualized.

Glossary

Akashic Records   Information of our past, present, and future lives said to be stored on Alcyone, one of the stars of the Pleiades.

Ascension   When the physical and energetic bodies reach higher dimensions without going through the death process, or when the cells of the physical body increase their vibration and can no longer remain in a physical state.

Astral body   The exact etheric double of the physical body, which leaves the physical body when we sleep and travels to the astral and higher planes; it is said to be connected to our solar plexus by a silver cord.

Astral plane or realm   The nonphysical realm of consciousness, which corresponds to the physical world but is not of it. There are said to be seven levels of the astral. The lower astral level is commonly known as "hell" and the higher level is known as "heaven."

Aura   The luminous energy field surrounding any living thing, which is generated from its light-body and form. The aura forms the bridge between the physical body and light-body.

Aztec   An ancient term referring to Mexican people.

Baktun   A period of 394 years in the Mayan calendar, 13 of which make the Long Count.

Cellular memory   Memory of all experiences that is held in our cells.

Chakras   Vortexes of energy within the etheric field of the body. There are seven main centers through which higher-dimensional energy is introduced to the physical body. Each main chakra is linked to a main gland.

Channeling Information coming from other dimensional sources and transmitted to the third-dimension.

Christed self When the consciousness of the earthly self combines with the higher Self and has access to other multidimensional selves.

Collective consciousness One mind of a group; the gathering and uniting of minds.

Conscious The ability to be guided by higher intelligence, such as being guided by higher levels of our Self. Being aware of our multidimensional selves.

Conscious self See "Small self."

Dimension Realm in which physical or energetic realities manifest; each dimension is a higher frequency than the previous one.

Electromagnetic field Energy field generated by electricity in magnetic fields.

Enlightenment Liberation from the lower self and from the restrictions of the third dimension; a reconnection with Source/God.

Etheric body Closest body to the physical, which acts as a filter between the physical and all other energetic bodies.

Fifth dimension A higher-dimensional level where our light-body and our Christ consciousness reside.

Frequency The rate of the vibration around all living things.

Galactic center The center-most point of the galaxy.

Galaxy A vast formation of plasma clouds that contains a large system of stars.

Gnosis The ability to "know" without physical evidence or proof. Derived from the Gnostics.

Higher Self An extended part of our self, living in a higher dimension; the link between our conscious self and our soul.

Home   When we leave the confines of the physical body and return to the higher dimensions.

Interdimensional   Crossing from one dimension to another.

Interuniversals   Highly evolved super-intelligent beings and energy forms that exist and travel between universes.

Karma   The sum of all our individual experiences, past, present, and future.

Light-body   An energy body that exists at a higher level, closer to the soul. Opens portals to the higher realms of light and connects us with the universal mind.

Lightworker   Individuals who have incarnated on Earth from throughout the universe to help with the ascension of humanity and the planet.

Long Count   Period of 5,125 years of the Mayan calendar. It began August 11, 3114 BCE, and will end December 21, 2012.

Luminous energy field   See "Aura."

Luminous Ones   Higher dimensional Beings of light. Great spiritual teachers for humanity. Highly advanced guides and masters who overlight humanity and work in service of human and planetary evolution through spiritual channels located on the Earth plane.

Mayan calendar   A calendar said to have been given to the Mayan people by the Pleiadians, with an end date of 2012.

Metaphysics   The branch of philosophy dealing with the nature of existence.

Milky Way   Our spiral-shaped galaxy, home to billions of stars, including our Sun.

Multidimensional selves   Many aspects of ourselves that reside on different dimensions.

OBE   Out-of-body-experience, when the consciousness leaves the confines of the physical body.

Olmec   The mother culture of the Mayan civilization.

Paradigm A model of reality shared by a group of people.

Pleiadians Fifth-dimensional beings from the Pleiades star system, who are far more advanced than humanity, having already attained Christ consciousness.

Portal A doorway to different dimensions.

Precession The circular movement of the Earth's axis.

Precession of the equinoxes Axial precession imparts a "wobbling" motion to the rotational axis of an astronomical body, causing the axis to slowly trace out a cone. In the case of the Earth, this type of precession is also known as the precession of the equinoxes. The Earth goes through one such complete precessional cycle in a period of approximately 26,000 years, during which the positions of stars slowly change.

Psychic attack An "attachment" or "possession," when an outside energy imposes its will upon a living human being. When one is "attacked" in waking or dream time by external astral entities and energies.

Quantum physics The study of energy that exists in units that cannot be divided: very small quantities of electromagnetic energy.

Shaman A person with the ability to contact and see other worlds and dimensions.

Small self The third-dimensional ego self or "personality," living in the physical world of duality and separated from higher Self.

Soul The immortal part of oneself.

Source God. God Mind. ONENESS. The eternal force. The eternal state of "Is-ness" without end. The very Beingness of God.

Star gate See "Portal."

Third dimension The physical world anchored in a linear time- and space-based reality. The reality where human consciousness resides.

Vibration The oscillation and movement of a particle. All creation is manifest from divine energy. Everything physically manifested vibrates within certain ranges of frequency. The density of a living organism governs how fast that energy can physically vibrate.

Resource Directory

The organizations and resources listed below have been selected as those that provide important ideas, support, and inspiration in empowering us to help transform the current global system.

CONSCIOUS EVOLUTION

These individuals and organizations represent inspirational new-world thinkers working at the cutting edge in the arena of the evolution of consciousness. While this list certainly does not represent all the possible people and organizations in this area, you may find the work and ideas of those listed below particularly useful in assisting the evolution of your own consciousness.

Individuals

Bruce Lipton
www.brucelipton.com
An internationally recognized authority in bridging science and spirit who has been a guest speaker on dozens of TV and radio shows, as well as keynote presenter for national conferences.

Byron Katie (The Work of Byron Katie)
www.thework.com
The Work of Byron Katie is a way of identifying and questioning the thoughts that cause all the fear and suffering in the world.

Carlos Barrios (The Maya Mystery School)
www.mayamysteryschool.com
The Maya Mystery School of Northern California is an educational network whose purpose and goals are to relay information about the coming 2012 time

shift as recorded by the ancient Maya, to inform the public as to how the Maya and the Mayan sites will play a key role in the preparation for this 2012 shift, and to network with like-minded organizations and entities that are applying the teachings of the ancient mysteries as interpreted by the Maya.

Damanhur
www.damanhur.org

Damanhur is an eco-society based on ethical and spiritual values, awarded by an agency of the United Nations as a model for a sustainable future. Damanhur promotes a culture of peace and equitable development through solidarity, volunteerism, respect for the environment, art, and social and political engagements.

Eckhart Tolle (Eckhart Teachings)
www.eckharttolle.com

Eckhart's profound yet simple teachings have already helped countless people throughout the world find inner peace and greater fulfillment in their lives. At the core of the teachings lies the transformation of consciousness, a spiritual awakening that he sees as the next step in human evolution.

Ervin Laszlo
www.ervinlaszlo.com

Ervin Laszlo is generally recognized as the founder of systems philosophy and general evolution theory, serving as founder-director of the General Evolution Research Group and as past president of the International Society for the Systems Sciences. He is the author or editor of sixty-nine books,translated into as many as nineteen languages, and has over four hundred articles and research papers and six volumes of piano recordings to his credit. His current work focuses on prospects for Humanity's future and the interconnecting cosmic field that underlies all. Ervin Laszlo is Founder and President of the Club of Budapest (www.clubofbudapest.org).

Gandhi
www.mkgandhi.org

Comprehensive site that is regularly updated and maintained by non-profit Gandhian Organizations in India, providing a wealth of information about Gandhi, his life, work, and philosophy.

Geoff Stray (2012: Dire Gnosis)
www.diagnosis2012.co.uk

A database for information about the year 2012 with information from scientists, artists, mystics, alternative Egyptologists, prophets, divinatory systems, shamanic psychonauts, mythology, and Mesoamerican research.

Giordano Bruno GlobalShift University
www.giordanobrunouniversity.com
A humanistic online institution committed to creating informed and ethical agents of change who bring a new consciousness, a fresh voice, and up-to-date thinking to the global community, transforming obsolete paradigms and empowering the co-creation of an equitable, responsible, and sustainable world.

Gregg Braden
www.greggbraden.com
For over 22 years, Gregg Braden has searched high mountain villages, remote monasteries, and forgotten texts to uncover their timeless secrets. Combining his discoveries with the best science of today to offer fresh insights into ancient mysteries.

Jasmuheen (Cosmic Internet Academy)
www.selfempowermentacademy.com.au
Dedicated to the co-creation of personal and global health, harmony, and peace by supporting the fulfillment of the Embassy of Peace Programs and Projects.

John De Ruiter (College of Integrated Philosophy)
www.collegeofintegratedphilosophy.com
John de Ruiter simply yet sublimely answers any heart that has honestly longed to live for what is real. Exposing the fundamental distortion within human consciousness, John gracefully unveils the immanent living way of Truth.

Jose Argüelles (Foundation for the Law of Time)
www.lawoftime.org
The Foundation for the Law of Time is dedicated to the cosmic mission as one human family is to define and exemplify the principles of a genuinely planetary culture of peace based on the mandate for a new time. This mandate is fulfilled through the 13 Moon/28–day calendar, the harmonic timing standard of natural time that transports us into the new evolutionary era, the noosphere.

Jude Currivan
www.judecurrivan.com
A cosmologist, planetary healer, international award-winning author, visionary, and educator, Jude works worldwide aiming to empower others, raise

awareness and facilitate practical and sustainable harmony, cocreativity and wholeness. As a cosmologist she has scientifically researched the universe at its most minute and mighty as well as the universal wisdom of many spiritual traditions.

Stanislav Grof
www.stanislavgrof.com

A psychiatrist with more than fifty years experience researching the healing and transformative potential of non-ordinary states of consciousness. His groundbreaking theories influenced the integration of Western science with his brilliant mapping of the transpersonal dimension.

Thomas Hubl (Sharing the Presence)
www.sharingthepresence.com   (NOTE: This website is in German. Click on the UK flag in the upper right corner for the English version.)
Thomas Hübl is a contemporary spiritual teacher. His workshops and trainings invite people to experience a deeper dimension of self-awareness and individual responsibility.

Wendy Webber (The Heart of Change)
www.heartofchange.org

Wendy Webber has been working in the field of personal and social transformation for over 25 years. She trained and practiced as a transpersonal psychotherapist for many years in the UK, where she founded a Center for Harmony, Health, and Conscious Evolution.

Organizations

The Centre for NonViolent Communication
www.cnvc.org

A global organization that supports the learning and sharing of NVC and helps people peacefully and effectively resolve conflicts in personal, organizational, and political settings. The NVC community is active in more than 65 countries around the globe.

The Findhorn Foundation
www.findhorn.org

A spiritual community, ecovillage, and an international centre for holistic education, helping to unfold a new human consciousness and create a positive and sustainable future.

The Foundation for Conscious Evolution
www.evolve.org

Widely regarded as Buckminster Fuller's philosophical heir, Barbara Marx Hubbard is a social innovator, speaker, author, educator and pioneering leader in the new worldview of conscious evolution. In 1990 she cofounded the Foundation for Conscious Evolution through which she developed the Gateway to Conscious Evolution, a global educational curriculum enrolling participants in the developmental path toward the next stage of human evolution.

Four Winds Society
www.thefourwinds.com

An international research and training organization that is preserving a thousand year old tradition of knowledge to achieve personal and planetary healing. Founded by psychologist and medical anthropologist Alberto Villoldo, their mission is to train master practitioners in the shamanic wisdom and healing arts of the ancient Americas.

Global Project Delphis
www.earthtrust.org/delphis.html

A conservation effort to save wild dolphins as well as an international dolphin behavior and cognition research project.

International Sufi Movement
www.sufimovement.org

Founded by Hazrat Inayat Khan with the following objectives: to realize and spread the knowledge of Unity, the religion of love and wisdom, to discover the light and power latent in man, the secret of all religion, the power of mysticism, and the essence of philosophy, without interfering with customs or beliefs, and to help to bring the world's two opposite poles, East and West, close together by the interchange of thought and idea; that the universal brotherhood may form of itself, and may meet with man beyond the narrow national and racial boundaries.

Miracle
http://whitebuffalomiracle.homestead.com

Official website for Miracle, the Sacred White Female Buffalo. Not an albino, she was considered to be the first female white buffalo calf born fulfilling a 500-year-old prophecy. She was extremely important to the religious beliefs of many American Indian and Canadian First Nations tribes.

Pachamama Alliance

www.pachamama.org

A U.S. based not-for-profit organization that was born out of a relationship developed between a group of people from the modern world and the leaders of remote indigenous groups in the Amazon region of Ecuador.

Positive TV

http://positivetv.tv

Looks to reach across generations and energize us with positivity at a time when we may feel overwhelmed by the negative prognosis for the future of humanity and the planet. In covering all aspects of human activity Positive TV looks to broaden the global conversation and raise questions about the world we live in and what sort of future we want to create.

Sacred Mysteries

www.sacredmysteries.com

An Ancient Mystery School for the Modern Age which uses DVDs and the Internet to re-create the ancient experience of "Mystery Schools" to teach the secret mysteries of the ancients such as: how to navigate through the spiritual realms, how to divine the future, healing through breath, wholesome plants and dream work, well as the power of the spiritual disciplines of sacred geometry, ritual work, and meditation.

Spiral Dynamics

www.spiraldynamics.org

Programs are concerned with why we cooperate, collaborate, and come to conflict over differences in values and the deeper value systems that form them. Provides options in charting differences in leadership, learning, management, social structures, economics—and virtually every other area where human thinking has an impact—and how to cope with those differences more effectively.

The Tao Centre

www.taoistcenter.net

Promotes a simple, natural, nonhurried, spontaneous way of living. Shows that life's unfolding patterns of yin and yang energy serves to nurture all life in its profusion.

Tibetan Buddhism
www.dalailama.com
Official website of the Office of His Holiness the 14th Dalai Lama.

WorldShift Movement
www.worldshiftmovement.org
A Movement "for the people" to cocreate a peaceful and sustainable world on behalf of all the people and the Earth. Calls forth humanity to unite in the cocreation of Peace, Compassionate Justice, Sustainability, Social Innovation, and Conscious Evolution.

WorldShift 20
www.worldshiftcouncil.org
The Worldshift 20 Council is composed of twenty prominent global citizens from diverse cultures and religions worldwide. The mission of the Council is to give urgent attention to the new condition of the world emerging today and provide essential orientation so that an informed and determined movement toward a peaceful and sustainable planetary civilization can be brought into being.

WorldShift Media
www.worldshiftmedia.org
Promoting Peace, Justice, Sustainability, Social Innovation, and Conscious Evolution

HEALING THERAPIES AND PRACTITIONERS FOR ALIGNING OUR PURPOSE

There are many healing practices and therapies that can help accelerate our path to wholeness and integration. Listed below are just a few of the options that provide support to heal the body, emotions, mind, energy, psyche, and soul.

Astrologers

Julia Bondi
www.juliabondi.com
Julia has been an accomplished counseling astrologer, intuitive, teacher and writer for more than 30 years. With degrees in clinical psychology and esoteric philosophy Julia brings insight, clarity and caring to her work.

Marcus Mason
www.heavenandearth.org.uk
Exploring and understanding the ever-changing relationships between the Spiritual and Earthly aspects of our Being, through the lenses of Astrology, Crystals, Acupuncture, Earth Mysteries, Shamanism, and Seasonal Cycles. Offers courses, workshops, meditations healing, readings, sacred journeys, and sacred ceremonies.

Attachment Releasement Organizations

Ian Lawman
www.ianlawman.org
Exorcist and Psychic/Medium, Ian Lawman can bridge the gap within the two planes of existence to prove that life goes on after death via detailed messages of past, present, and future.

Spirit Releasement Organisation
www.spiritreleasement.org
William and Reverend Judith Baldwin are widely regarded as pioneering experts in Spirit Releasement Therapy, removal of demonics, recovery of soul-mind fragmentation, and past life therapy.

Healers

John of God/ João De Deus—The Miracle Man of Brazil
www.johnofgod.com
João Teixeira de Faria, internationally known as John of God or João de Deus, is arguably the most powerful unconscious medium alive today and possibly the best-known healer of the past 2,000 years.

Mediums (all offer telephone readings)

Anna Kaye
www.destinydoctorannakaye.com
An International Psychic Medium, Soul Mentor, Reiki Master/Teacher, Metaphysical Teacher, Intuitive Counselor, and Life Coach. (Orginally the Destiny Doctor intuitive psychic agony aunt with *Vision Magazine*.)

Donna White
donnatelephone@aol.com
The extraordinary Medium who predicted this book and saw Miracle around me.

Psychospiritual Healing

EFT–Emotional Freedom Techniques
www.eftuniverse.com
A simple yet remarkable healing system that reduces the stress that underlies much disease. It works on a variety of health issues, psychological problems, and performance issues, even those that have been resistant to other methods.

Raymon Grace
www.raymongrace.com
A native of the Appalachian Mountains of Virginia who has been studying forms of healing since 1973. He is founder and president of Raymon Grace Foundation and has taken dowsing to new heights, empowering individuals to gain more control of their lives. His work has been used in at least 10 countries to improve water quality, reduce violence in schools and communities and to eliminate abuse of women and children.

Sacred Healing Art

Alex Grey
www.alexgrey.com
The official website of visionary artist Alex Grey.

Lorrie's Angels
www.lorriesangels.com
Lorraine Coffey is a spiritual artist whose journey of discovery has taken her from her homeland of Ireland to the mystical and ancient lands of Southern France. On this website you can discover the Angels that Lorrie has painted throughout the years and discover the range of Gifts for the Soul, which you can order through the website.

Luke Owen
www.lukeowen.com
Luke Owen's artwork is powerful, emotive, challenging and honest, and never fails to evoke an emotional response in the viewer.

Sound Healing

Jonathan Goldman
www.healingsounds.com
Jonathan Goldman, in conjunction with many dedicated and visionary people, has spent the past three decades working to bring the healing nature

of sound into mainstream awareness. On this site you will find: Articles & Interviews, an excellent Bibliography as well as Vibratory Research. This material focuses on many different aspects of sound including: resonance, psycho-acoustics, entrainment, toning, harmonics, chakras and mantras.

Tom Kenyon
www.tomkenyon.com
Tom Kenyon is a teacher, scientist, sound healer, psychotherapist, musician, songwriter, singer, shaman, and author. His life studies and many lifetimes of remembrances, complete with background knowledge and experience allow him to move with equal facility between Tibetan Buddhism, Egyptian High Alchemy, Taoism and Hinduism, and the sciences relative to each.

Unisonic Ascension
www.unisonicascension.com
Provides products that blend the science of music therapy and audio psychology to assist with healing and regeneration, using a combination of inspiring music and binaural beats that enable effortless relaxation and deep meditation.

Transpersonal Psychotherapy

The Karuna Institute
www.karuna-institute.co.uk
The Karuna Institute is an international residential Training and Retreat Centre. All the activities of the Institute are based on mindfulness practice. As such, Karuna is one of the oldest centers worldwide to integrate and teach mindfulness practices as professional healing skills in the West.

The Psychosynthesis and Education Trust
www.psychosynthesis.edu
The longest established psychosynthesis center in Britain. The Trust's vocation is to address the needs of humanity in a way that is pragmatic as well as spiritual and relevant to everyday life, acknowledging both the pain and potential in the human experience.

RETREAT/WORKSHOP CENTERS

Grail Spring's Retreat for Body, Mind, and Spirit
www.grailsprings.com
The focus is *Lifestyles of Health and Sustainability* for people and planet,

where one can reignite good health, energy, passion, and be deeply inspired to live a spiritually fulfilling life.

WorldShift Peace Retreat
www.worldshiftmovement.org
A place to "retreat" from the normal demands of life, in order to pause, breathe, take stock, re-evaluate, rest, recuperate, replenish, re-nourish, and resource. Caters specifically to those whose vocations and lives thrust them to the forefront of the world peace movement, as well as those who actively campaign for a better world or whose work involves them in helping humanity.

SPIRITUAL BUSINESS CONSULTANTS/COACHING

Matteo Baronti
www.matteobaronti.com
Matteo Baronti utilizes his unique Perceptive Coaching tools and techniques to facilitate breakthroughs for individuals that result in living a life without self-imposed-restrictions or limitations, making it possible for the experience of a consistent state of well being.

Janice Haddon
www.janicehaddon.com
An Executive Coach, with a focus on leadership development, stress management, and well being, Janice Haddon also utilizes a unique Business Strategy Diagnostic that enables organizations to drive through the change agenda, accelerate performance, and successfully integrate business strategy, people strategy, and culture.

Robert Pino Center for Growth
www.robertpino.com
Robert Pino, strategist, executive coach, TV host, and medium, works with people and organizations from all over the world to help them to get to the next level. His approach consists of using strategy and metaphysical talents and down to earth techniques to reveal your moment of truth, to formulate the necessary steps to go through a sustainable positive change, and to teach you how to achieve personal freedom.

Ethical Website Development / Promotion

Pure White Consulting—Internet and Business Consultants
www.purewhiteconsulting.co.uk
An independent Internet and Business Consultancy based in London.

About the Author

Nicolya Christi is an author and an advocate for peace whose work focuses on humanity's next evolutionary stage of consciousness. Nicolya is the founder of WorldShift Movement (www.worldshiftmovement.org), inspired by Ervin Laszlo, and is a co-initiator of WorldShift 2012. She is a spiritual guide and facilitates large "Gatherings" in which she and her team work with high-dimensional spiritual beings (who she refers to as The Luminous Ones) to help accelerate the human evolutionary process. At these events, she works with dialogue, individual and group process and journeywork, attunements, and powerful "transmissions" to catalyze an acceleration of consciousness and an elevation of personal frequency. In certain individuals, this process can activate the natural evolutionary transformation from *Homo sapiens* to *Homo luminous*.

For details of Clarion Call seminars, talks, and online courses, visit:

www.2012aclarioncall.com

To register for a Residential/Non-Residential *Transformational Journey into Conscious Evolution* or *Awakening the New Human—from Homo sapiens to Homo luminous* course, to host one of these events, or to invite Nicolya to attend one of your events, please visit:

www.nicolyachristi.com

About WorldShift Movement

WorldShift Movement has been established specifically for *the people* to join together to co-create the foundations of a new world built upon peace, compassionate justice, sustainability, social innovation, and conscious evolution. This makes it unique in the arena of "better world" initiatives.

WorldShift Movement seeks to actively engage people in co-creating a new world based upon the highest human values and principles including equality, inclusivity, forgiveness, empathy, compassion, co-creation, cooperation, cosupport, collaboration, nonmonetary transactions, nonviolent and compassionate communication, and unconditional giving and receiving, as prerequisites for establishing the essential foundation upon which to build a world in which peace and sustainability are lived realities for All.

An ongoing series of high-profile campaigns, events and activities, which enlist *the people* and engage evolutionary thinkers and prominent global personalities have been planned, dedicated to establishing peace, societal transformation, and ecological restoration worldwide. Details can be found on the WorldShift Movement website.

The primary objective of WorldShift Movement is to call forth humanity to NOW unite and co-create a new world through collaboration in ongoing campaigns and events as well as various media outlets.

WorldShift Movement campaigns for humanity to become both individually and collectively empowered to establish new social, economical, ecological, and environmental values and systems that will ensure a peaceful and sustainable future for all of humanity now and for future generations. By uniting as One Voice, we empower ourselves and each other to become active guardians of all life and of the Earth.

WorldShift Movement is an ever-growing team of dedicated WorldShifters, including eminent scientist, author, twice Nobel Prize nominee, founding father of WorldShift, and author of *WorldShift 2012,* Ervin Laszlo.

Please visit our website to read about who we are and what we are doing, to join us and become part of the WorldShift Movement working team as a volunteer or a supporter.

WorldShift Movement—*A Movement of its Time and for the People*
www.worldshiftmovement.org

WORLDSHIFT HUMAN EVOLUTION CENTRE

WorldShift Movement is seeking land in central Europe, ideally Southern France/Rennes le Château, or in California/San Francisco for a WorldShift Human Evolution Centre.

The center will offer residential personal transformation programs supporting the creation of inner peace and the cocreation of world peace through psychospiritual development, conscious communication, and conscious evolution. Programs will include psychotherapeutic one-on-one and group journey work, the raising of vibration and frequency, activating the lightbody, DNA activation, right and left brain balancing, and super/higher conscious (channeled) communication with extradimensional energies within the context of the cocreation of peace on Earth. A specialized program to activate and support the conscious transformation of the Self and the human body from *Homo sapien* to *Homo luminous* will also form part of the curriculum.

Visiting evolutionary leaders, indigenous shamans, and medicine women/men will offer workshops and events in conscious evolution, karma to dharma, healing of ancestral, past, present soul trauma imprints held within the luminous energy field, clearing invasive energies and entity attachment, connecting with the Earth and Heavens, soul retrieval, future Self manifestation and psycho-energetic development. The WorldShift Human Evolution Centre will also maintain a strong focus on the Arts.

If you would like to help manifest the
WorldShift Human Evolution Centre, please contact:
info@worldshiftmovement.org

THE WORLDSHIFT PEACE RETREAT

The WorldShift Peace Retreat offers a place to "retreat" from the normal demands of life, in order to pause, breathe, take stock, re-evaluate, rest, recuperate, replenish, renourish, and resource. It requires no working contribution from those who stay, instead offering an unconditional, sacred space in which to just let go. The Peace Retreat caters specifically to those whose vocations and lives thrust them to the forefront of the world peace movement, as well as those who actively campaign for a better world or whose work involves them in helping humanity.

For more information, please visit
www.worldshiftmovement.org

Index